SUPPOSED TO FLY

Books by Miroslav Holub
in English translation

POETRY

Selected Poems (Penguin Books, 1967)
Although (Jonathan Cape, 1971)
Notes of a Clay Pigeon (Secker & Warburg, 1977)
On the Contrary and other poems (Bloodaxe Books, 1984)
The Fly (Bloodaxe Books, 1987)
Vanishing Lung Syndrome (Faber & Faber, 1990)
Poems Before & After: Collected English Translations
    (Bloodaxe Books, 1990; reissued, 1995)
Supposed to Fly (Bloodaxe Books, 1996)

PROSE

The Dimension of the Present Moment (Faber & Faber, 1990)
The Jingle Bell Principle (Bloodaxe Books, 1992)
The Long Disease (Milkweed Editions, MN, 1996)

SCIENCE

Immunology of Nude Mice (CRC Press, Boca Raton, Florida, 1989)

MIROSLAV HOLUB

SUPPOSED TO FLY

**A SEQUENCE
FROM PILSEN,
CZECHOSLOVAKIA**

Translated by
EWALD OSERS

BLOODAXE BOOKS

Copyright © Miroslav Holub 1996
Translator © Ewald Osers 1996

ISBN: 1 85224 274 4

First published 1996 by
Bloodaxe Books Ltd,
P.O. Box 1SN,
Newcastle upon Tyne NE99 1SN.

Bloodaxe Books Ltd acknowledges
the financial assistance of Northern Arts.

Cover printing by J. Thomson Colour Printers Ltd, Glasgow.

Printed in Great Britain by
Bell & Bain Limited, Glasgow, Scotland.

It's a river that carries away, but I am the river.
It's a tiger that destroys me. It's a fire that consumes,
but I am the fire. The world, unfortunately, is real.
I, unfortunately, am Borges.

JORGE LUIS BORGES: *The New Refutation of Time*

Acknowledgements

Supposed to Fly was first published in Czech under the title *Ono se letělo* by NAVA, Pilsen, in 1994, marking the 700th birthday of the city of Pilsen:

The photographs in this Bloodaxe edition are by four photographers, whose initials appear after the captions: F. Dosttál, V. Radechovský, V. Škarda and M. Hauner.

Some poems which now form part of this sequence from Pilsen are reprinted from Miroslav Holub's *Poems Before & After: Collected English Translations* (Bloodaxe Books, 1990), including some translated by George Theiner drawn from earlier collections. All other translations in this book are by Ewald Osers.

Contents

11 Supposed to fly
13 *The bird*
14 The vertical city
16 *Certificate of baptism*
17 The curtain
18 *Home*
19 The summer-house
21 *The roof over our head*
22 The airfield
23 *Behind the house*
24 On the essence of lyric poetry
25 *The geese*
26 On the origin of the Spejbal puppet
27 *Punch's dream*
28 When you aren't looking
31 *Memo to a pre-school-age daughter*
33 Journey into the depths
35 *Cinderella*
37 The bard
39 *End of the game*
41 The theatre paradox
45 *A history of the world*
46 On fencing
48 *A helping hand*
49 Pocket Christmas
50 *How to paint a perfect Christmas*
52 The crib
55 *Liturgy*
56 Escalation
57 *End of the week*
58 The kilometre
60 *Magnetism*
61 The park
62 *Spinal cord*
63 Snakes
64 *Two in a landscape*
65 Man in the park
66 *A dog in the quarry*
69 The zoo or about suffering

70	*Consent*
71	Butterflies
73	*Boy catching butterflies*
74	That day we entered life
75	*We'll go up the tower*
77	The Germans
78	*Herbarium*
79	The station
80	*Five minutes after the air raid*
82	Manon
83	*The parallel syndrome*
84	Bombs
85	*The bomb*
86	Identity
90	*The fall of Troy*
91	How the beast of war lay down
93	*Interferon*
99	The fraction line
100	*The day of the Pollyanna*
101	On the phenomenon of the family zither
102	*Pietà*
103	The horses
105	*The searching tram*
106	The fowl
107	*Anatomy of January*
108	The city under the ground
110	*The old people's garden*
111	Bridges, footbridges and souls
114	*The map of Europe*
115	Darkness
116	*The duties of a dustbin*
117	The secret life of steam locomotives
119	*Tender souls in tough bodies*
120	402 muskets
123	*Executions*
124	'Haven't you heard, you dumb cattle?'
127	*Central cemetery*
128	The metaphysics of beer
129	*Pompeii*
130	Fragrances
132	*Reading*
134	Deukalion's people

135   *On the origin of football*

136   Aida

137   *Mother is learning Spanish*

138   Winds

143   *Half a hedgehog*

145   The triumph of death

146   *Requiem*

147   Wenceslas II only just made it

149   *Good King Wenceslases*

150   What to ink out

153   *Masterpiece*

159   BIOGRAPHICAL NOTE

This book is a little like a musical suite. A suite is a sequence of short compositions which can stand on their own but feel happier when they're together. And as a rule they're in the same key.

The key here is provided by the well-known saying of the Good Soldier Švejk: 'I like it when someone comes directly from somewhere.'

Because some of the pieces were written many years ago, and that original 'from somewhere' clings to a person and flows through him like a sap, like lymph, it should be stated here that some of the poems have appeared in English translation before. The rest of them I wrote recently, with a great awareness of a debt owed to Josef Hrubý and Josef Koenigsmark, who planned a book of this kind in 1969-70, but I then only managed to write the title (a different one) before the shutters came down on all good fellow-citizens.

M.H.

The author at a time when he conceived this book,
not yet suspecting that one was supposed to fly.

Supposed to fly

At the famous parliament of birds in Budějovice it was decreed to hold a speed-flying competition, in fact a race.

Who will be the first to get to Prague, to the Old City Square that has always been the scene of great historical events, such as the execution of sundry German and Czech noblemen or the airbrushing of a certain Party secretary out of a balcony group photograph?

The frigate-bird flapped its wings in the Budějovice square and, *frrr*, they were off.

The first to reach the Old City Square, as everybody knows, was the swallow. Next the martin. Then came the eagle, the goshawk and the hobby. Then the starling, the blackbird and the bullfinch. The seagull and the heron. The wagtail and the bluetit. The bunting and the yellowhammer. The jay and the magpie. The lark and the warbler. The barn-owl and the eagle-owl. The wren and the kingfisher, according to how the wind blew.

When they were all present, as listed in Janda's *Natural History*, when the drug tests had been completed (much simpler with birds because of their cloaca) and when all the participants had been handed their diplomas, the crested lark noticed that the pigeon was missing.

The raven declared that this wasn't kosher and they must make sure he wasn't trapped in a net, which would invalidate the race. So they all flew back again. The buzzards, the kestrels, and the falcons surveyed the route with their sharp eyes. Benešov – nothing. Votice – nothing. At Putím at last something white. The birds made their descent into a stubble-field, where they found the pigeon strutting about.

Where the hell have you been, pigeon? the stork exclaimed reproachfully. We've all been to the Old Town Square and back, and no trace of you anywhere!

Oh, said the pigeon, one was supposed to fly?

So much for the little anecdote. Even though I don't see any significant difference between a proper anecdote and solid literature as long as this literature doesn't suffer from mental flatulence and wind.

So much for the little anecdote. And although I am absolutely not responsible for my name – which, of course, means pigeon in

Czech – a name I didn't give myself and which, I'm told, goes back to the Přibíks of Klenové, who probably were a fine lot of birds because they didn't even establish a West Bohemian picture gallery in their castle, I can't help admitting that I rather like the idea of being a bird strutting through a stubblefield.

Whenever I think back to Pilsen, which now lies ten or twenty or thirty or forty years back, I always have a nagging feeling that the others all flew and I, alas, never noticed.

The bird

The bird that pecks the seconds.
The bird that swallows the minutes.
The bird that digests the hours.

The memory bird which
restores to the present
the bell's long-drowned sound.

The bird trapped in a paper
bag, the bird caught on the bird-lime
of tears, the bird beating its wings
in the deep dungeon of books,

the bird as a slave of writing which
itself is the slave of memory,

the bird which wiped out
the fourth dimension of the landscape
and now twitters in the gut,
the little skeleton bird, the brittle
dirty thorax bird,
the matted-plumage bird,
the agnail bird,

the bird because of which there'll never
be peace again.

The vertical city

It is nonsense, of course, that a person is born in some town. He is born in some kind of beaker of air that is gelatinous with a metallic ring and rattle. It is like being suddenly unsheathed against direct light and robbed of all nocturnal stars.

All round him, first of all, emerge four pillows, then four bedsides and finally four walls with a gas lamp at the top. It is an Antarctic trek and the shipwreck thirsts for blood.

Around the four walls labyrinths slowly emerge. Alleys. Gateways. Passages and canals. A few Minotaurs roaring from a great distance. After a certain eternity it is a house and down there below the window opens the vertiginous chasm of the backyard, where toys may be thrown which are a little later brought back again, gnawed by rats. Toy houses and little green fences with traces of rats' sharp teeth. And so we have a merger of rodents which are called rats and chasms which are called fairy-tales.

Then Škréta Street emerges.

Slowly pavements multiply, pavements of granite flagstones, all the way to the railing round the thick shrubbery by the train stop in the southern suburb from whose store-house of horrors now and then erupts a train.

Only then does geodesy begin with a raised hand which grabs a big hand higher up. Geodesy leads to the self-generation of further streets, which evidently were never here before, of blocks, and of a very special kind of street down which tram cars tinkle and squeak. These streets stretch further day by day until they reach the square. Or the park.

Simultaneously with this growth of squares and parks comes the ruin of Škréta Street, which has ceased to be the only one, and a many-voiced hubbub of people of different blood, who are more numerous than ourselves and who overlap like film frames later constituting both action and subtitles.

It's terrible, but out of all that emergence and hubbub and film-frame there is eventually sown the seed of what one day will be called your native city, that something which will grow and grow until the day when it shrinks into the beam in thine own eye.

The city therefore grows with everyone and pulsates and vanishes and grows again and no one ever comes from it but it comes from everybody. Toddling or posthumous.

There isn't one horizontal Pilsen. There are ten thousand vertical Pilsens, which were born of us. So long as we don't believe that Pharaoh's daughter fished us out of the Nile.

There is one Pilsen belonging to one person. He threw it out of the window, but they brought it back again, gnawed by the rodents which are called rats.

When Apollo flayed Marsyas he sent the children out into the street. [VR]

Certificate of baptism

Date of birth – date of baptism.
The pendulum clock wound up,
the case locked, to make sure
the door doesn't fall out.
Matrimonial bed, denomination
under both species, so the wine shouldn't go sour
during the autumn storms. The chaplain as black as a blackbird,
Aspergillum, matins.

Seven pounds,
skin pink, slightly icteric,
hair downy. And howl.
Age two million five hundred years.

By old age we reduce this
to a few hundred,
because for more we no longer
have the guts.

The curtain

Any kind of personal recollections inevitably end up as a piece – a chunk – dross – a literary spore as soon as we arrive at the conviction that, by our own relentless hard work, we have made our way in the world and that the young people of today do not appreciate their divine gift and that the conditions of our childhood may have been hard, but honest and closer to the soul than today's supersonic flights and the flushing of lavatories with the Watersave system. Which reminds me that Thomas Alva Edison's family in their house in Milan, Ohio, didn't have a loo at all but went out into the garden, even though the inventor doesn't mention this fact in his memoirs.

I certainly don't believe that Pilsen was beautiful or close to the human soul; on the contrary, as my mother kept pointing out, the city had resisted the Hussites, which went against the spirit of Czech history, and, what was even worse, in my day it had a Red at the town hall, i.e. the Social Democrat mayor Pik, which went against the National Democratic soul of my father and allegedly of all decent people generally.

I was in fact gently brought up anti-Pilsen.

Besides, my childhood circumstances were neither hard nor sentimental, but cotton-wool-wrapped and equipped with a garden, and with two lavatories, albeit unheated ones, which delayed my way in the world. Nevertheless, in the upstairs lavatory one was faced with an off-white curtain printed with little brown squares with little brown dots inside them, in unending rows and columns, horizontally and vertically.

I would count them in both directions, moreover with a vague sense of being also slightly anti my own and seemingly present childhood.

I would sometimes count up to two and sometimes up to three hundred and guess how many little squares with little dots there were in one column including the turned-in hem, in one fold and in the total area, if they were as many as the stars in the sky or houses in Pilsen, or little boys in the world, or all children sitting on the loo at that moment, or all people who ever lived.

Infinity, as represented by the square-patterned curtain, impressed me profoundly and regularly. It was, on the one hand, a transcendental curtain and on the other a relativistic one.

By its insoluble problem it suggested that it should be of no great importance how many there are of one thing or another, anti what we are brought up or where we end up, with our finiteness.

Home

From amidst last year's cobwebs
she glanced up from a creaking easy-chair:
'You're looking well, boy.'

And wounds were healing,
we were children again,
and no school today.

And when things were at their worst,
with no night and no day
and no up and no down
and we barely dared breathe,

she'd say
from amidst her cobwebs:
'You're looking well boy.'

And wounds would heal before her eyes
even though she was

blind.

The summer-house

It isn't true that in the pre-first-world-war, post-first-world-war and pre-second-world-war garden suburbs at Lochotín, Slovany and Bory the more or less well-heeled bourgeois only built villas, chalets and little houses in the spirit of the poet's words – which they didn't know: what would we be without those seaman's dreams. Just because of those dreams of distant lands they not only built villas. There were magnolias. Box trees. Tulips. Narcissi called asphodels, because that's what Edgar Allan Poe liked. Mosses like Mr Šedivec at Bezovka near us. Currant bushes. Garages. Lilies. Lilacs. Rows of dahlias and Virginia creeper on ornamental walls.

To complete the work they built summer-houses, for those sailors' dreams.

A summer-house is more than human work. It is human to build a roof over one's head or over one's car. Thereafter we build a summer-house as a roof over a hero's idea. The idea is that we are more than we are, that we have more than we have, and that we will feast on some beef broth before it gets cold in a corner of the garden. A summer-house is man's great dream, which (in his mind) he draws like a Chinese poet in Indian ink, although in reality he's calculating how many sausages he can buy for Saturday.

A summer-house is the great dream of merging with deciduous nature without having to roll in the grass, where in August there could be chiggers. A summer-house is the dream of the last emperor, who was cast out on to the island of one garden.

The summer-house is the personal germ of the Tower of Babel, cut short in its evolution like the coccyx. Nonetheless the germ of 'making a name' for oneself, as the Bible puts it. Kafka said about the Tower of Babel that... one might perhaps hope that the next generation will pull down what's been built and start afresh... – which is the *Ur-geist* of the summer-house. Or is the summer-house the township which, according to Kafka, arises instead of a towering structure and just for the time being. And if for the Tower of Babel the significant, or indeed the crucial aspect was its natural non-completion, its abandonment, its abortiveness, its resignation in advance, then the summer-house, strictly speaking, is not only a germ but also the final stage of a tower shrivelled like the mummy of an obese monk.

Our family also built a summer-house. One Sunday on the edge of history we lunched in it on beef soup and cutlets with lettuce, and that was the end of it.

After that it was used as a depository for litter, literature, lino-leum, liquorice, liquor-bottles, leaf-mould, linocuts, little stuffed buzzards and lifelong vain hopes. The summer-house became the flute of a wailing wind.

The summer-house became an abode of hopelessness upon which the rain began to fall. It became the ruin of a fortress that conquered itself. It became a domain which no one was going to steal from us because it had become alienated from its substance.

The boundless pathos of the Czech summer-house would deserve a mention in the national anthem and in the coat of arms.

Our cities consist essentially of our summer-houses, of which only few survive as shelters, as improvised chicken coops for shit-covered hens kept illegally and listed as eagles.

And if in past centuries they built summer-houses in our cities as pig-sties straight away, with the result that our cities stank worse than many others in Europe, the principle was still the same, because not even three urban pigs need have stunk quite as much if we devoted ourselves to them as much in the second year as at the moment of installation and not as if they were summer-houses.

A summer-house is a great metaphor of existential oddity. If we don't have cities, towers and houses, then a summer-house will spring up anywhere in our flat, acquiring the shape of a side-board, a corner behind a tapestry, an idyll with grannie and china, a book-case or a music centre. A summer-house in classicist style, or *fin de siècle*, or *empire*, or more often rococo or from the spiritual period of early-republican or late post-Bolshevik baroque.

I warmly remember our house, both during the day and in my dreams – that is, I remember the summer-house as a headless decrepit statue of innate futility.

The roof over our head

No sooner does a human head develop
than there sprouts over it
the purple necessity of a ceiling, a cave
or a mole hole.

Because we know from centipedes
that there are always enough feet to get somewhere,
but sometimes not enough feet
to get back again.

Lightning from the gods' leather quiver
furiously drums against the tin roof,
giving rise to a profile of the house
and an approximate portrait of
father and mother.

And in the black hole at the world's end
will be a poppy-seed embracing all
caves and buds and shelters,
as well as the collapsed summer house in our garden,
the weakest point of our already defeated
thatched defences.

Let the burghers' houses be tattooed and furnished with escutcheons, for
sick demons and scruffy angels to live behind them. [VR]

The airfield

The Bory airfield is overgrown with grass and cow-pats. On an afternoon walk, in our Sunday best, we collect them, now properly dried out, father in his attaché case, mother in her bag, I in my school satchel. Father, proudly erect, looks all round to make sure no one sees us, either from the penitentiary or from the hangars.

It's something like original sin and I am deeply ashamed before the face of the archangel, whose head peeps out from the gravel-pits behind the hangars.

The cow-pats are to turn into garden manure in a barrel, but they never do because they always get full of bugs and spoil.

These are the consequences of sin. From the Noseks over the fence the scene is watched by the motionless eye of a hen, which is closed by a triangle.

Which is why we go to the airfield again and yet again. The hangars smell of some kind of heavy oil.

However, a dark biplane trainer is taxiing up to the hangar. As it turns towards us the roar of its propeller is like the roar of a charging Shir Khan and there is no escape. The sky is split open and the parents are helpless.

We are alone, as in a dream in which one takes off heavily.

He who takes off heavily always flies furthest, says the poet.

No doubt the poet must have collected something himself to conceive such an idea.

Behind the house

Behind the house is a leaky saucepan of destinies.
A scooter grown wise with age.
On a clothesline a wisp of stale breath.
Nitrogen oxide. A drop of blood.

And in the shed in a heap
rags, ropes, rumpuses
and angels.

On the essence of lyric poetry

In the attic, behind its heavy tin door, a little haunting went on, especially after dark, I mean those long snake-like tapeworms that wind around beams with eyes goggling, while round the corner plump, rapacious feathered chickens are playing peep-bo.

In the cellar there used to be a goose in a crate, which was stuffed three times a day with roasted bread-rolls. Without anaesthetic, the roll was simply dipped in water and the goose was knelt on.

When the cellar door was opened the goose below quacked softly and lyrically. She was alone in that wash-house and she was pleased to hear someone coming.

I believe that this was and is the very essence of lyric poetry.

The geese

In hesitant file
between cottage and heath
they strut and seek
what cannot be found.

Week after week
one by one they disappear
and white feathers swirl
through the kitchen air.

In hesitant file
those left once more waddle
keeping the empty space
swaying
in the middle.

Week after week
between cottage and heath
each one of them hopes
with its final breath:

now this time quite surely
the goose world will change
and with wings extended
far and wide we shall range.

With wings extended
far and wide we shall range.

On the origin of the Spejbl puppet

The lights are turned off and on the stage of the little 'Theatre of vacation camps' appears the land of Havilah, where there is gold. Saint Hurvínek and Spejbl converse in a mumble. Like being beyond time and space.

Everybody laughs, which is the better alternative to saintliness.

The burning bush burns without being consumed.

Spejbl rides in a car, Punch is on a horse. The Parrot is on a motorbike. Hoho, rejoices Spejbl in a deep voice because the brollie is lying on a brightly coloured operating table and Old Ma Škrholová comes in with cakes. There's a hedgehog in the hedge maple.

Tiresias' breasts on threads.

Enter the Princess.

The curtain falls. Off-stage the puppets, as they are hanging up there, are still out of breath.

When a semi-detached was built on Mánes Street the Nosek sisters took the northern half because there was a wheel-barrow on that plot. We have the southern half without a barrow. The Nosek sisters have a Nosek brother, with whom they don't live in saintliness, even though in the ceilar he carves his puppets and hangs them up in the window to dry, the window giving on the garden.

Five Spejbls, eight Hurvíneks, wood-naked, barely breathing.

Mr Nosek is picking cherries from a tall old tree, under which stands the barrow. The sisters, who aren't living in saintliness, take his ladder away. The Nosek brother screams from the tree, exceedingly loud with a lot of unfamiliar expressions, evidently from plays which haven't been written.

This goes on till late at night. Down below in the window the wood-naked Spejbls wave their white legs in the thickening dusk. They'll probably catch a cold.

Punch's dream

I'll slip out in front of the curtain, taking
great care not to tangle my strings
in the flies,
I'll jingle my bells (merrily),
doff my cap
and before the puppeteer knows what's happening
I'll speak in my own voice,
you know,
my own voice,
out of my own head,
for the first and the last time,
because afterwards they'll put me back in the box,
wrapped in tissue paper.
I'll say what I've wanted to say
for a whole eternity of wood,

I'll say it, no matter how ridiculous
my little voice may sound, how embarrassingly squeaky,
I'll say the most important, the most crucial thing,
I'll speak my piece...

Maybe it will be heard.
Maybe someone will take note.
Maybe they won't laugh.
Maybe it'll grow in the children
and irritate the grown-ups.
Maybe it'll change the colour of the set.
Maybe it'll rouse the cardboard
and the spotlights' shadows. Maybe it'll shift
the laws of relativity.

I'll say...Hi there, kids, you're a great bunch,
say hello to your pal Punch!

When you aren't looking

You know of course that it would be a terrible waste of images, sounds, petrol, solid fuel, mental energy, hormones and electricity if cities were to move all the time, functioning, growing and going to seed, constantly, ceaselessly and continuously, even when you aren't looking.

When you aren't looking there's no reason for anything to happen, because there'd be no proof that happening had any meaning. Not only no meaning but no record. Unrecorded happenings would be a decay of energy, happenings unobserved by you would be pure entropy brought to its total end.

Not only does an observer affect his observation, but an observer gives meaning to what he observes, thereby lifting it out of the depths of meaningless and empty idle running or no running at all. Between the last two no perceptible difference can be established.

History is only what someone has witnessed. If nobody witnessed it then it ran idly, or it didn't run at all, in which case it is impossible to distinguish between these two alternatives, so that in effect they aren't alternatives at all.

A tadpole which no one has seen is a non-tadpole. A moth which no one has seen does not exist and in vain beats against the window, producing a non-sound. In this way, as we all know, several thousand species of animals, cryptogamous plants, blue algae, viruses, sprites and little souls become extinct on our planet every day.

This fundamental aspect of reality was already understood by our myth-generating ancestors...

The Olympian gods and the knights of the Holy Grail were moving between the state of the invisible and the state of the visible. In the state of the visible they entered into happenings, sagas, epics and destinies. In the depths of the pure, meaninglessly and idly running invisible they had to be furnished with a shining glaze, so that one at least could lament over them.

This was very clearly stated by a hundreds of years old fairytale maker. The Sleeping Beauty with all her fittings became operational, including her basic biological functions, as for instance, spinning, kissing, reviving the castle and producing fertile progeny, merely as the result of being seen by an accidentally passing prince. Without having been seen she would have finished up by disposal and absolute non-usability like some never discovered trilobite.

This basic aspect of reality we all of us grasp sometime and somewhere. Someone as a barely born babe, someone else as a superannuated grandfather.

I had to admit this to myself very acutely the moment I surrounded myself with Pilsen.

If you walk down Fodermeyer Street, right at the corner of Andělská the Brouk and Babka department store is brought into operation, people walk in and out, carrying parcels or not carrying parcels, a child pulls a tricycle and an aunt lugs a rubber hot water bottle, the cash registers tinkle and on the shelves the merchandise is having a good time. A little way down towards the square the Meinl store at once hits you with its fragrance of coffee and a black boy with a tall red fez steps on a display board.

As you go in the shops they begin to do business and in the flats they begin to live. The tram to Slovany begins to move down Zbrojnická Street and people with shopping bags and milk-cans begin to wait at the stops.

The grumblers are beginning to grumble and those who have fainted or suffered a heart attack are beginning to be carted off.

The moon is beginning to rise, as you go, and at six they begin to let down the shutters. Sounds are beginning to float around and someone remembers the history of kindness, the manufacture of pig-iron, kicking into stones and speaking Czech.

If you don't go down Fodermayer Street but instead take Mánes Street, you'll see old-age pensioners walking their dogs and dogs walking their old-age pensioners, while shadows and shit-heaps thicken. Lilacs are beginning to smell and here and there a Praga car rattles past.

While in Fodermeyer Street everyone steps into the store of images and waits for the stage-prompt bell.

If you're riding a bike from Doudlevce to Slovany you have to reactivate the pines and the spruces on Homolka Hill, so that their trunks should begin to develop new annual rings while at the final stop of the tram the pointsman switches his points with a billiard queue. In the highrise blocks the lights go on in the windows and in the pubs they're beginning to draw 12-degree beer. While in Bory they're making for the image store and wait for the bell.

When you're at school your home is put away in a little box like the wooden castle with its battlements and the family is tipped in like silver-painted plaster knights...When you're at home, school shrinks into a painted wooden pencil-box and Mr Tolar the teacher turns into greenish-yellow chalk.

That's why you are fully and totally responsible for what happens and what doesn't happen.

You're responsible for the fact that on the hill behind Božkov stands the Radyně ruin and that lumps of masonry are falling from it. You're responsible for the fact that the train is going to Kotěrov and that they are carrying someone to the Central Cemetery in a black hearse.

We Pilseners are responsible for Pilsen, even if the last house were to crumble. If it crumbles we should have looked at it. Then it wouldn't have done.

His soul had approached that region where dwell the vast hosts of the dead ... – wrote James Joyce in *Dubliners*. He was thinking of the State Science Library. [VS]

Memo to a pre-school-age daughter

When no one's watching
behind us
the sky and the rain are rolled up
like music paper with a trumpet part,
houses and squares are tidied away in a box
padded with newspapers,
the birds change into letters
in a secret black book,
puddles reflecting night and distant
fires are stowed away in the attic
like grandfather's presents to grandmother.

The trams are put away in cotton-wool clouds.
Pedestrians go to the cloakrooms
and unwrap their sandwiches:
their walking is over
when no one's watching.
And through the city, on seven long legs
a giant spider stalks and in a whisper
advertises the next scene.

It's interval time in the dubious theatre
of a thousand actors and one spectator.

When you're elsewhere the home left behind
shrinks to a blown-glass crib
under a superannuated Christmas tree.
Dogs with eyes like teacups
and dogs with eyes like millstones
carry off your princess
from the gloomy castle, where
philosophers stand on their heads
and the king puts away his crown,
too heavy for a fool.

Flocks of other children rise
into the branches of the ancient elm
and twitter as they fall asleep.

When you're elsewhere the home behind
is soaked up into a small mirror
and our parents act in a theatre of flies
of which you're unaware because it is
a play within a play
and night's about to fall.

That's why I always cried a little
when we had detention
and home was not in sight.

But now I have got used to it.

Even though
I still don't know the play.

Journey into the depths

Every Sunday I used to undertake a journey into the depths of time – this was on our family outings to Rokycany, Šťáhlavy, Šťáhlavice or Nezvěstice. By train, of course, since we had privilege tickets. These outings seemed to me exceedingly wearisome, always the same track, always the same forests, always the same stones. Rather like the labour of Sisyphus, assuming that Sisyphus, even before pushing that rock uphill, also had to drink a pint of full-cream milk, which was half churned by the train journey, so he'd feel sick at least on the way up.

These outings forced me to find some entertainment for myself, both in daydreams of becoming a famous painter, a collector of butterflies, or finding a brand-new trilobite in the gravel, and in gazing at things. In the course of such gazing I discovered some mounds and hillocks the size of petrified ant-heaps of super-ant dimensions immediately behind Kozel Castle, but also further on and deeper into the beechwoods. Mother instructed me that these were the burial mounds from long-ago burials of long-ago mound-burial people from the Hallstatt period, which was thus called because no one really knew what period or what people they were.

And so, while scrabbling about in the stones, I reflected on how, in the depth of the earth, there were the skeletons, vessels, arm-bands, horses and carts of people who croaked from some Hall-statt disease or other people, who, in order to prevent those Hall-statt diseases, sacrificed some Hallstatt subjects, little slaves or lit-tle prisoners, sometimes ritually eating their victims under the beeches of another generation, and generally exhibited many other customs by which the Stone Age culture shuffled over into the Bronze Age and Iron Age cultures. It was a comforting thought that all this prehistoric shouting, horror, hideousness and ripple of bared muscles has fallen so prettily and lyrically silent after those 2500 years, crystallizing into little bones, beakers, buckles and chains under layers of clay and under the slow descent of golden leaves. How violent prehistory transforms itself into gentle instructive material suitable, or indeed recommended, for all young boys and girls.

And I reflected that from these mound-burial people we also derive some sort of basis of our own existence, even though, according to the *Book of Czechoslovak History*, Sphinx Publishers, Bohumil Janda, intermingled with Celtic Boyans and ethnic Marcomannians and Quadians, who of course successfully butchered and raped the Slav tribes pouring in from the east, fleeing from some Hunnish nationalists, those Slav tribes of whom it isn't even certain whether they were red-headed or dark-haired, brachycephalic and tall or square-built; until eventually from this primeval goulash mix there emerged our own pigeonesque, peaceful, character.

Turning the pages in that Czechoslovak history, I found that in our Pilsen basin, at the confluence of four rivers, not even those Slavs were really clear-cut. Everywhere they had tribes with impressive names – Kharvatians, Zlichanians, Lemusians, Lutomeritians, Luchanians, Pshovanians, Dechanians – but we were merely a kind of outcrop of Slavs who'd rolled on too far, of Czechs intermingled with Luchanians from the Mže valley. We didn't even succeed in having our own dialect – according to a Professor Matiegka in the history it was just vaguely 'south-western'.

We didn't even have anyone to exterminate – no Slavníkovians and no missionaries, we didn't even have any fratricides or enemies of public order, only a few filthy robber barons and a little trading with towns in Bavaria.

We didn't even get a mention from Jirásek, that long-winded writer of historical legends.

I sincerely hope that now when we celebrate the foundation of New Pilsen by Wenceslas II in 1295 some pure ethnic trait and anthropological characteristic will be discovered. But having successfully graduated from the Czechoslovak State Classical Grammar School in Huss Street, I have always firmly believed that, by comparison to Southern Bohemia, we don't really exist at all and that, with the exception of the Chronicle of Troy, printed in Pilsen about 1468, we have just been culturally, ethnically, linguistically and folkloristically loafing about, that we didn't crystallise in terms of religion either, that somehow we've been historically illegible, so that it was found more appropriate to do Wallenstein to death in Cheb, since in Pilsen conditions were too confused to take any historic action at all.

And that's also why historical literature has been in an even worse state with us, since, according to Henry James, the production of a little literature requires a lot of loafing about by history.

Cinderella

Cinderella is sorting her peas:
bad ones those, good ones these,
yes and no, no and yes.
No cheating. No untruthfulness.

From somewhere the sound of dancing.
Somebody's horses are prancing.
Somebody's riding in state.

The slipper's no longer too small,
toes have been cut off for the ball.
This is the truth. Never doubt.

Cinderella is sorting her peas:
bad ones those, good ones these,
yes and no, no and yes.
No cheating. No untruthfulness.

Coaches drive to the palace door
and everybody bows before
the self-appointed bride.

No blood is flowing. Just red birds
from distant parts are clearly heard
as, plumage ruffled, they alight.

Cinderella is sorting her peas:
bad ones those, good ones these,
yes and no, no and yes.

No little nuts, no prince that charms
and we all long for mother's arms,
yet there is but one hope:

Cinderella is sorting her peas:
softly as one fits joints together
with fingers gentle as a feather,
or as one kneads the dough for bread.

And though it may be light as air,
merely a song in someone's head
a gossamer of truth is there.

Cinderella is sorting her peas:
bad ones those, good ones these,
yes and no, no and yes,
no cheating in this bout.

She knows that she is on her own.
No helpful pigeons; she's alone.
And yet the peas, they will be sorted out.

The bard

I believe that the *genii loci* have all died out – there is no time for them in our age. The action and scene changes on our stage proceed helter-skelter, and before you've got used to one Punch another has popped up and the prompter is carried out dead from the wings.

When I was in my primary school in Chod Square there were still at least some local bards. In our neighbourhood, Bezovka, we had a live and kicking local poet of our Chod region, Jindřich Jindřich – a circumstance which I greatly appreciated, to the extent that I felt we should all act a little like Chods and speak, and perhaps even write poetry, in Chod dialect. If I'd realised that this was essentially a matter of regional identity, I'd have even tried to get hold of an appropriate costume, as I had seen on the curtain of the theatre, painted by Augustin Němejc, or, after it rose, on the members of the choir as they intoned Let us all rejoice together, that opening number of the *Bartered Bride*, under the watchful eye of Mr Barták, the conductor, so that it was impossible to say whether they were rejoicing more in those yellow leather trousers and lambskin caps or in the approving glances of the conductor.

Anyway, though only wearing civvies, we had rehearsed with Mr Tolar, our teacher, a few of Jindřich Jindřich's songs and on the occasion of the Master's (roughly) fifty-fifth birthday (at that time the figure seemed to us a particularly praiseworthy achievement of senescence) posted ourselves in the courtyard of the two-storey house in question and, accompanied by our teacher's violin, intoned our piece. Mr Tolar was tall and skinny, he had a small moustache and a suit with a waistcoat, and during his artistic performance a massive vein stood out on his forehead, which I regarded as a measure of creativity. At a signal from his bow we burst into devoted song, something like See the child greeting you, O native Chod tongue, and the vein on Mr Tolar's forehead stood out like a weal, and he played and waved his fiddle like Paganini playing the Devil's Trill and I felt that we were ascending towards the regional angelic choirs, so I howled even more devotedly, even though Mr Tolar had told my mother that with my musical ear a pianissimo would be preferable, and we yelled O native Chod tongue like wolves howling at the moon and our teacher fiddled away and we all gazed up at the second floor for the Master to appear and descend by parachute or at least join in our chorus with the enthusiasm of Verdi's *Nabucco*.

After a few verses the great man really did appear, though only ephemerally, rather like President Beneš at Prague Castle during the student demonstration in 1948, but then he probably had good reasons. The Master parted the curtain and waved his hand to us, very much in the manner of Tsar Nicholas in the St Petersburg theatre.

Mr Tolar bowed deep with his violin and bow in his hand and we stood staring at the Master and at the curtain and our Chod identity seemed to evaporate instantly from our consciousness.

All that was left to us was Chod Square, which admittedly, with its technical college, our primary school, God's little church with the peeling paint on its towers, and the shapeless little park, was as close to the Chod tradition as a fiddler crab is to Vivaldi.

The loss of Chod identity affected me so deeply that I determined to compose my own Chod song, making use of the family's Petrof grand piano and my acquaintance with musical notation, learnt from my piano mistress Helena Matoušová in Dobrovský Street, who would rather give me theoretical tasks, while my grades in piano playing fluctuated within the limits of musical tolerance and my lesson copybook was dominated by exclamations 'Fee received with thanks!' My greatest pianistic achievement was the adroit catching of a standard lamp knocked over by my lady teacher in her emotion at my rendition of Rachmaninov.

Nevertheless I composed my 'Chod Song' for one voice without accompaniment and throughout two weeks regarded it as profoundly inspired.

End of the game

When the ball had rolled away
and come to a halt
against the black thread of evening,

a little boy,
a fat little boy,
on whom they would place
an owl's head,
so they could again have
the old post in their fence,

walks through a black gateway and
a grey courtyard,
discovers the ciliary motion
of the scattered stones
and broken boards,
out of the corner of his eye he watches
the mating of the old stairs into the cellar,
the silent dance of carbon,
the dry tears of the washtub,

the little boy,
the fat little boy,
on whom they would place
the head of Punch,
so he should nod and
tinkle his bells
at encounters,

rides on the old spinster tram
and on the train, her
eighty-year-old cousin,
does not spit on the floor
or lean out of the window,
does not pull the communication cord even though
he can hear
cries
        for help,
some cry for help

from the inside of the earth,
even though he sees
the empty sky,
only slightly outlined by jet planes,

the little boy,
the fat little boy
with his leaking
piggy-bank of a heart

looks out of the window
at the immense simplicity of the world,
at ruins and new buildings,
at open doors and
closed doors,
at jolting
   and silence,
yawning mainly from pubs,
the detonation of cobwebs,

he's humming
a fat little song,
conversing
with the mouse angel of home,
opening a compound picture book
of Punches and owls.

Even though he feels
that he'll have a long way
to return
to the future.
Even though he feels that,
like a grand word,
like a small round taste of blood
in his mouth,
a wisdom tooth is growing,
that tooth
which most people so far
have had to have extracted
as they grew old.

The theatre paradox

There isn't only the acting paradox. Before it, first of all, comes the theatre paradox. This consists of the fact that we call some building a theatre if it has a cupola and some statues of hardy naked types with helmets atop it. Inside there is a surfeit of a terrible emptiness of gilded fossils, baroque, and purple plush, in which even the museum carpet-beetle pegs out.

The auditorium is filled with a vacuum that chokes every flame voice or mouse, down the corridors drifts a strident violin note or the muted C string, conjured up by an absolutely forlorn scorpion which in desperation eats the carpets and suspends itself from the hangers in the cloakroom, pretending to be a plastic raincoat that someone left behind.

In this inflated emptiness under the name of theatre the theatre under the name of performance becomes an unlocking of various glass doors, of echoing footfalls, of a putting on of overcoats by cloakroom attendants with their bags of cakes and tea, of the admission of deviant citizens arriving early, of a visit to the toilets and of the occupation of the auditorium by intending spectators who don't see the numbers or don't understand the numbers on their tickets, with the result that they sit down wherever the Good Lord guides them, except that the Good Lord then sends a ticket-holder with the correct number, but only after the third bell and the dimming of the house lights, and the one who has sat down where the Good Lord guided him establishes with the help of the flashlight-armed ticket attendant that, Good Lord or no Good Lord, his ticket is for Tuesday and for the first-tier balcony which then raises a hum and a muted noise such as reigned before Troy when the Achaeans secretly planned that wooden horse which was nothing else than the first theatre without the use of a stone building.

An auditorium furnished and inhabited by a chocolate-munching public is something so existentially different from a row of seats covered with a dust-sheet, in order to preserve the plush. For the Nation and People, that the brutal question has to be asked whether the raising, pulling-aside or disappearance of the curtain, either of fabric or just light, and the entrance of the actors and the plot signify anything more than confirmation that some people have arrived and are now waiting for something that will eventually be described by the local critic as a theatrical performance rehearsed by the guest director. Paradoxically, the theatre doesn't begin on the stage, but with the hanging up of one's overcoat in the cloak-room and the placement of a person or persons in their seats or standing room.

I am able to make these observations because I used to be the theatre expert of our grammar school, in consequence of which I knew how much more could be seen from the stalls in rows 1 to 3 at 9 Crowns each than from the seats in rows 4 to 7 at 5 Crowns each, and because I used to make propaganda for *The Secret* or for *Our Swaggerers* or for that nineteenth-century Klicpera play *Hadrian of Rheims*, during which a nude female above the gateway on the backdrop was always covered with a bed-sheet to make sure the students didn't get any immoral ideas. I routinely applied the universal argument Grab yourselves some culture, you cretins!

Myself, I made full use of one complimentary ticket for every ten sold and was a fanatical follower of the May Events, when the Pilsen Opera became faintly international by employing among others the Danish tenor Tyge Tygensen and by getting some guest performers from Prague, among whom Jaroslav Gleich engraved himself on my heart not only as the Prince in *Rusalka* but also as a Pinkerton in *Madame Butterfly*, who fearlessly on his thin shanks carried the Butterfly of Mme Kočová – who, to tell the truth, had on her a little more than the sixteen years prescribed by the libretto as well as a good nine stone – off-stage for a passionate purpose and to grateful applause.

There was another occasion when I perceived the paradox of the theatre. I was then still a child and was being taken by my parents to a performance of the Prague *Osvobozené Theatre* which had come to Pilsen for a guest performance. Miroslav Horníček, actor and fellow Pilsener, may also remember that in *Chalk and Cheese* the actors came on stage from the auditorium by a little bridge over the orchestra pit, and so Jan Werich, making his way to the stage between the stalls and the boxes, suddenly stopped to ask some city dignitaries in a box if they had any chocolates. The family looked embarrased. Werich then turned to the audience – where at that point all argument stopped about who had a ticket for now and who for Tuesday or for the balcony – and uttered the memorable sentence: Look at them, they got themselves the box and had no money left for chocolates.

It was a theatrical beginning which confirmed that it wasn't a beginning, but that it had begun when the box holders and stall holders turned up, or indeed when they put on evening dress and a tie that wasn't too shabby, slipping a bag of goodies into their handbags or right pockets. It emphasised the theatre paradox which makes a blushing toff in a box equally important as Jan Werich, even though their real distance is of the order of the distance between a soft-centre chocolate and a philosopher.

Another consequence of the theatre paradox, of course, is the sorry state of the theatre everywhere, from Pilsen to Minneapolis-St Paul, where they haven't got Jan Werich and where the artists pretend that the play starts with the curtain up. That it is just a problem of lines and a problem of the stage set, and not a problem of the auditorium which is so strongly reminiscent of Heraclitus's river.

In front of the theatre on Sunday afternoons was the students' corso – So often a beloved hand/brushes our heart with gentle touch/and makes our heart bursts its steel band…wrote Sully Prudhomme on the subject. [FD]

A history of the world

First there was hydrogen,
then helium,
the fourth state of matter,
and then gas,
and then water,
and stone.

Then there was protoplasm
running through the fingers of
the angel of death.

Then pithecanthropus
roasted a rabbit.

Later Břetislav
defeated the Hungarians
and carried off Jitka.

In the end Mother
ruled a black copy-book
and wrote it all down:
there it all was
with dates and loving
notes at the bottom.

Many boxes remained empty.

I'm trying to fill
some of them.

Except I don't know if I'm doing so
because the world still
has so many blank spaces

or because
Mother left them
in that black
copybook.

On fencing

In the Municipal Entertainment Hall they were holding the Mandl Memorial Fencing Tournament. Master Kunt, tall, gaunt, bald and who was imprisoned after the demonstrations in 1953, had instilled in us Pascal's and Rilke's belief that sport without technique is the wreck of the body and that technique without morality is the wreck of the soul.

That everyone who weeps in this world weeps for us.

That everyone who laughs in the world...

In consequence I believe that sport exists chiefly so that we can say that my own ball was out and my opponent's just clipped the line. I believe to this day that there is a substantial difference between a sportsman in the Anglo-Saxon sense of the word and a crooked sportsman in the East European sense.

At the Mandl Memorial Fencing Tournament I was one of the judges. On the piste were Master Skýva and Master Marschal. By the side of the piste stood a little table with the trophies; the black money, if there was any, would be in one of the smaller rooms next to the Assembly Room. But most probably there wasn't any.

Master Marschal attacked with a *flèche*, but tripped up and found himself with the upper part of his body under the little table with the trophies, outside the piste. In sabre fencing a hit is good if it is above the belt, both front and back, provided the hitting man has both feet on the piste. The person hit can be anywhere in the world.

Master Marsál was wriggling under the table with the trophies, backing out, supporting himself with the sabre he was still clutching. Master Skýva was waiting on the piste, and as soon as Marsál's back hove into view, with his jacket riding up, exposing his bare skin, Master Skýva struck. There is a gentleman's agreement in fencing that one does not strike when one's opponent has lost his weapon. Marschal had not lost his weapon, he was merely crawling backwards from under the little table with the trophies. The hit was valid and I had to raise my hand.

But I can still see Master Marschal's eyes. The hit must have been hellishly painful on his bare skin. But that was not what his expression was about. It was about something outside the rules. Even outside fair play. Even outside political screening, original sin and collective guilt. Even outside that dignity which sometimes commands us not to kick a man when he is down. That expression was about the loss of elegance.

Sport without elegance is the wreck of a dream, let's say the dream of victory.

In the Pilsen Sports Club we were taught not only by Master Kunt, but before him by Master Táborek, who was a little over seventy, and by Master Kulhánek, who was eighty and whose hand was shaking in the 'mailed fist' positions between tierce and quart. His legs weren't up to much by then, but his hand was still quick. And elegant.

Sport, just as art, originates when we become aware of a mandatory elegance.

Otherwise it would merely be a question of wealth, merit and weals on the back.

A helping hand

We gave a helping hand to grass –
    and it turned into corn.
We gave a helping hand to fire –
    and it turned into a rocket.

Hesitatingly,
cautiously,
we give a helping hand
to people,
to some people...

[GT]

Pocket Christmas

The Christmas Tree of the Republic used to stand in Republic Square, loudspeakers would pour out amplified Christmas carols, large snowflakes would be falling, the church spire would be piercing the soft underbelly of the sky, and vertical and horizontal expectations would fill the old city to its crusty edge. There were collecting boxes for the poor, the blind, the deaf, the visually impaired, the lost and those not yet found, and everyone who tinklingly or rustlingly made a contribution was given a lapel label with a pin. They were coloured – white one day, yellow the next day, pink the third day, blue the fourth day and a paradise colour the fifth day because those were the days when some twenty kilograms of a person landed on the scales of some twenty kilograms of hope.

On the pavement in front of the lavatories – which are out of order to this day – stood an experienced unshaven crier... Every sparkler... Brilliant and bright... In a different colour... And with different light... That's it, ladies and gentlemen, every single sparkler... Brilliant and bright.

The tram came along, ringing with the bells of the Second Book of Moses.

As youths we would walk there with some pretty girl we'd picked up in a bar on what was then called President Wilson Street. There were two of us and she had her right hand in my coat pocket along with my left hand, and her left hand with the other guy, that is along with his right hand. There was then no music audible except the music in my pocket. In Republic Square the music in my pocket was meaningful, but I had no evidence about the other guy's pocket.

This was a strange kind of pocket Christmas.

The gypsies turned their heads as we passed them. No one was selling sparklers any more.

But this Christmas was like a commemoration of the original Christmas with a tree reaching up to the sky.

Besides, Christmas is never anything other than a commemoration of an earlier Christmas, even though we may resist our habitual reductionism. Christmas is becoming more pocket-sized all the time.

Until all that's left in our pockets is our own lonely cold hand and the tiny little leg of some doll which I'd found in the street and felt sorry for.

How to paint a perfect Christmas

On top you paint
a sky as gossamer-thin as seaweed.
Below you pour on a little darkness
heated to room temperature
or a little higher.

In the dark a small tree will
scratch its way up with cats' claws,
the most beautiful tree
beyond the dreams of
all the world's forests.

And the little tree starts
shining by itself
and the whole picture sings
with green joy,
with purple hope.

And under that tree
you must now place
what is
most important,
what you most wish for yourself,
what crooners with guitars
call happiness.

It's easy for a cat.
A cat will put a mouse there,
a captain will put there
the biggest jet-propelled halberd
which can shoot, fire and salute,
a sparrow will put there
some blades of grass for its nest,

a bureaucrat will put there
a closed file tied with red tape,
a butterfly will put there
a new latex peacock's eye,
but what will you put there?

You consider, consider
till the daylight fails,
till the river has nearly flowed away,
till even the light-bulbs begin to yawn,
you consider
and eventually
in that darkness you blot out
a hazy white spot,
a little like a ducat,
a little like a boat,
a little like the moon,
a little like the lovely face
of another person,

a hazy white spot,
perhaps more of an emptiness,
or the opposite of something,
like non-pain,
like non-fear,
like non-anxiety,

a hazy white spot,
and you go to bed
and tell yourself:
yes, now I know,
yes,
next time
I'll paint
the best Christmas
ever.

The crib

In the church of the Redemptorists in Chod Square a crib would appear before Christmas, admittedly of plaster but richly painted, on a scale of 1:6 – assuming that angels in real life measure 1.80 metres, adorned with conifer branches and with an opulent background of the walls of Jerusalem or Bethlehem. It filled me with a strong pre-Christmas joy and a tension of several dozen volts, such as neither the pious if meek sermons from the altar nor the well-mannered instructions in the church vestibule were able to neutralise.

In front of the manger one little angel was turning a rather pimply face to the visitors and holding out a collection box. Whenever a coin was dropped into the box the little angel gratefully nodded his little head and pulled a red cord which led to a little bell in the little grotto, whereupon the little bell emitted a silvery tsink-tsink.

It was marvellous like the end of the Devonian period.

I did not doubt that the little treasurer angel well remembered how many coins a person had sacrificed and that, his on-duty time over, he'd report it in the poor plaster stable to Joseph the carpenter, the Virgin Mary and little Jesus in his small white swimming trunks.

Generally speaking, I did not doubt – and to this day do not doubt – the metaphysics of Christmas cribs in the right place at the right time.

Indeed, there are even more cribs than churches and chapels.

Above all, cribs are more powerful than the most elaborate and artistic thuribles. Walking through the Dalí museum in Figueras I regretted that the master didn't live to experience computer graphics and the electronic mastery of sculptures. Walking through the Picasso exhibition in the Museum of Modern Art I regretted that the master didn't have a clue about moon landings or the wonderful mice produced by genetic manipulation. Walking through the Miró gallery in Barcelona I regretted that the master didn't work with UV light and superoxide bursts.

I admit that I adopted these relativist attitudes as a result of the Christmas crib in the church of the Redemptorists. The masters move away from primeval wonder without coming close to the newest wonders. This is not, of course, just a case of my own eyes. It's a case of everybody's eyes, of those who have not used intoxicants to replace the natural catching of one's breath that was entrusted to all of us *in the beginning*.

I didn't understand – in art – how we could be further when we have forgotten how it was in the beginning.

Today I wouldn't give a coin to the little angel because I wouldn't know if it was not too small for him...I'd merely tell him this anecdote, which seems to me adequate to the original magic:

Well, as that comet was descending over the Bethlehem incident, Gloria in excelsis Deo, three kings arrive from the countries of the Middle East, carrying offerings of gold and myrrh, proudly erect. The first and the second king step up to the manger, bringing their offerings, accompanied by the grateful snorting of the little donkey and other unspecified livestock.

The third king, of taller stature, proudly erect doesn't pass under the low lintel of the poor stable but hits his head with a mighty crash, dropping his precious gift, grabbing his head and exclaiming:

'Jesus Christ, that was a bang!'

The Virgin Mary nudges Joseph the carpenter with her elbow:

'There you are, Joe, there's a name. Not Hugo, as you wanted.'

I have no doubt that the little angel would nod his head, ring his bell, and relate it after closing time.

Because I believe that even a little angel continues to develop and isn't a dry stick at all.

The number 29 tram ran round the Redemptorists' church and that wasn't a coincidence. Twenty-nine always was my favourite number and I believe that in the Prologue to Goethe's *Faust* there should be 29 angels, in the Walpurgis Night 29 monsters, and at the end 29 lemurs digging Faust's grave. [FD]

Liturgy

He climbed
the spiral steps
to the pulpit with the canopy,
looked around, saw glass eyes,
china ears, rosaries with threaded pearl-like
molecules of antibodies to words,

bowed his head and mimicked the stone
of the twisted baroque column in which
long ago Gothic silence had crystallised,

took a deep breath and immersed himself
waist deep into the organ pipes,
from which a muted minor-key cry for help
was seeping.

There was silence as if
just before an execution
the rope gets stuck.
It appeared that the cathedral
had sprouted a minaret like
a third hand which cannot close,
and at nightfall on the gallery
the muezzin wailingly intoned
Excuse me!

Escalation

When travelling to Prague we had a second-class privilege staff ticket. In those days there was still a third class. In Prague there were open sandwiches in Wenceslas Square, frankfurters in Celetná Street and Iphigenia in Tauris at the National Theatre. After the theatre it would be night-time and we would travel back by the train known as the nightbird, myself falling asleep on the train and howling in Pilsen, because after midnight it is always raw in Pilsen and frenzied Iphigenias chase along the track with horses' heads. Towards morning there is often even Tauris.

The next day, however, this satin-like escalation of the city, from Pilsen to Prague, was exceedingly stimulating and memorable. From Pilsen you could go places.

From Prague no longer.

An escalation of Prague would just be Paris, and that was already over-escalated. Paris was as if your toys had dropped into a canal under a northern-lights sky. There was nothing greater.

I see the beauty of life in that a 'more' is still possible, and for that Pilsen is just about right, at the beginning of the movement.

End of the week

The foundation of course is
the time-table which sometimes applies
from Monday to Friday, sometimes on Saturday,
and exceptionally on Sunday, when He rested
from all His works,

which we carry in a forgotten pocket
so that usually we miss our connection.

But we get there all the same.

It'll be Sunday again, the day of wilted songs.
In the first-floor window without curtains
a small girl will stand in a red dress,
waiting.

In the Spanish Square they will burn
eighteen Jewish Marranos
in honour of the marriage of Maria Luisa and Carlos.
We will not even stop
but go home by a back street,
deep in thought.

The kilometre

An avenue of gigantic beeches and ash trees and similar survivors of the Tertiary leads from Kalikovský's Mill to Lochotín Park, and according to legend measures exactly one kilometre.

A kilometre of boredom and miracles.

The river at Kalikovský's Mill breaks over a weir which, at high water, roars with a Palaeogenic voice and has the appearance of a full beard growing from one second to the next and then vanishing and moulting and vanishing and growing, and someone underneath roars angrily through a fluid mouth, if only because of that terrible transience. A flowing, dying, immortal Old Man of the Mountains.

Behind every tree lurks an Erl King, a Roc bird, a Jeroboam, a Stork-beaked ghost and a thief with a flat cap.

Autumn crocuses grow in the meadows and after dark you can hear the braying of donkeys, lions and Red Riding Hoods fed on Kalcit baby food. Cut into the tree-trunks are the signs of an indecent zodiac, without comment or explanation.

So many Erl Kings, tree trunks, donkeys and acts of licentiousness within the time of the European record in one-kilometre walking while holding hands. It'll never be broken, because nowadays a kilometre is, on the one hand, a lot shorter and, on the other, a lot longer.

Besides, endless prattle about one-kilometer avenues is either for senile old women or for geniuses which, in our latitude, are fortunately in short supply.

The spiritual core of a city are its statues. The best statue, as a rule, is some naked female. That's probably what comes first to a city's mind. [VR]

Magnetism

When the Queen, over the
magnetic lines of force
on Faraday's rough table, asked
And what use is it?
Faraday replied,
gazing lower than her
lace collar:

And what use, Ma'am, is a child?

It was a high point of science
in history, because

modern mankind is divided into those
who understand gravitation and those
who understand braces,

we either ask about everything,
or we ask about nothing,
in which case the universe originated
in the Square of the Republic
through the condensation of
Saint Nicholas's deodorant.

The park

Lochotín is one of those parks released into the landscape from Aladdin's lamp before it was stolen from him in some Russian town. The foliage of beeches and hedge maples rustles in the mirror-like air and a huge golden spider plays a probable tune on steel strings in the tree tops. It is a three-path park, triply divided like a fish-trap for dried fish, a three-movement quartet, or a treble helping of frankfurters on Sunday afternoon.

It is an epic park because it takes place within precise limits and every moment you come to its end, even though every park is by definition infinite and mythical, especially as the ancient trees always come up with enough ideas. Besides, in the lower part of Lochotín in an artificial grotto there used to be a genuine plaster hermit, behind a grille so no one should steal him, but eventually he was stolen all the same, just as that lamp, and replaced by non-mythical excrements.

In the covered pavilions under the trees the ghosts of Austro-Hungarian bandsmen are playing in full-dress shrouds, the conductor has white sideboards, and the benches at dusk are occupied by eighth-generation lovers who are waiting for it to get dark.

Otherwise all is deserted beneath the spiders.

Until one golden-shining day we walk along here with a girl whose soul, heart and breasts are no longer all that strange to us, and from the tree tops comes a melody, mind you, you can really hear it, perhaps they are having music at the hidden pub, in the pub we can't see, oh native land of hope and glory, as Seifert said, a tune as likely as the Rustle of Spring, as Sinding has composed.

In fact, ghastly kitsch.

But ghastly kitsch is the fabric of memories. And memories are the fabric of parks. And parks are the fabric of Never, never, nevermore and may the Lord have mercy on you as Nezval has written in his *Manon Lescaut*.

Spinal cord

Solomon's flute from elastic ivory,
organ pipes of white northern lights,
the song of dolphins and sirens,
the dorsal fin of a blind
cavern
fish.

Plaited Christmas loaves back home,
when instead of the mystery of baptism
what occupied me was
irregular Latin verbs.

An anthology of tenderness in Pascal language,

locked as always
into black rings
vertebrae
       vertebrae
              vertebrae,
because otherwise we would
from sheer immaculateness
be paralysed
straight after birth.

Snakes

On the rocky hillside above the Úhlava river there are narrow footpaths and beyond the river-bend towers the Valcha suburban railway station as if the golden fleece had been changed into small coin. On the rocky hillside there is also a wood and shade, and under the bench at the panoramic spot lies a used condom. Mother looks significantly at father, who tries to tread the condom into the ground. From the bench there is a fine view into the valley and as far as Litice among the distant fields.

We agreed that it was the sloughed skin of a snake. We always inclined towards science.

Except that I didn't know yet what paradise that serpent came from.

Mystery spread through the town as if the cocoon of a nun-moth had suddenly burst open. The town was getting more and more nocturnal. There was a hissing from the sleeves of darkness.

H.G. Wells's creatures of the night ate up the creatures of the day. Thus passed the years of Nevertheless and However.

However he eventually said to the serpent: We'll eat the fruit of the trees of paradise – and she came to the Alfa Cinema to see the Night Moth, where I had cunningly invited her.

We soon had the quietest path through the meadows well trodden and the sun had come within an arm's length. Thus also passed As Well As.

And one day the town began to shrink down to a single street, again as it happened to Škréta Street, to a single house in whose doorway we perform late-evening experiments similar to the removal of the wings of the Aztec winged serpent, which incidentally was incapable of flight, to a single flat, where there is a single girl –

The town shrinks into a single tiny spot at a writing desk, where under heavy drifting clouds a Ninth Elegy of Orten is written nine times to some Karina, who is still alive, where the only one is the only one – and roams I know not where, without ever arriving – which is all rhymed in Czech.

The town changes into a helicopter transporting a single body as if it were without a soul, as if it were a brain-dead body –

And thus we become serpents unto ourselves and the town is a kindred nest of vipers and every one of us is naked through the nakedness of the other and our hands are hostages unto themselves.

Anyway, what have you got against snakes?

Two in a landscape

In a bare landscape with dry vineyards
here and there a mammoth, overgrown with
newsprint like scales. A head in front
and another head at the rear. It watches us
intently.

In a wooden shack we lean with our back
against a rotten door. The trunk is approaching
through the gaping window. You protect me with your hair's shadow.
I protect you with an indigo-coloured whisper.

Nonetheless we return.
We return eternally,
head averted
against head erect.

Eyeball to eyeball.

Man in the park

The park at Bory belongs to that species of park over which there is always a transparent balloon or a Montgolfier balloon because the park is open towards the sky. From the loop where the tram turns back you come to the Linden Tree of Masaryk's Republic, later on just the Linden Tree when the republic had turned back on itself. It stands on the big scooter circuit, which proves that the Earth is flat.

The little greying benches have initials cut into them and on one of them beneath the poplar always lies a greying suicide in dirty clothes; they always remove him in the morning.

The chestnut trees in the hollow below the penitentiary bear spiky fruits similar to the golden apples of the Hesperides and a stone flung at the massive branches taps out a dry tune which rouses the hobbling park keeper to such an extent that he wheezingly curses and breaks into a run, in the course of which he usually loses one leg or a stick.

Other narrow paths are steep and covered in snow, providing a bumpy toboggan run while the German maid is necking with a soldier. The little train approaches from Litice. Finally there are also footpaths along the edge, under the flowering hawthorn, and with a girl with pink ribbons we walk through the hedge into the fields, where, admittedly, we don't quite know what to do with the ribbons or with the girl. Farewell, death, under the flowering hawthorn, wrote Mr Nezval. Farewell, goodbye.

The park is a place where one never knows precisely what to do. Except that one might find a lost leg, a Montgolfier balloon blown off course, or a few verses.

A dog in the quarry

The day was so bright
   that even birdcages flew open.
The breasts of lawns
   heaved with joy
and the cars on the highway
   sang the great song of asphalt.
At Lobzy a dog fell in the quarry
   and howled.
Mothers pushed their prams out of the park opposite
because babies cannot sleep
   when a dog howls,
and a fat old pensioner was cursing the Municipality:
they let the dog fall in the quarry and then leave him there,
and this, if you please, has been going on since morning.

Towards evening even the trees
   stopped blossoming
and the water at the bottom of the quarry
   grew green with death.
But still the dog howled.

Then along came some boys
and made a raft out of two logs
and two planks.
And a man left on the bank
a briefcase, in which bread is planted
   in the morning
so that by noon
   crumbs may sprout in it
(the kind of briefcase in which documents
   and deeds
   would die of cramp),
he laid aside his briefcase
and sailed with them.

Their way led across a green puddle
to the island where the dog waited.
It was a voyage like
   the discovery of America,
a voyage like
   the quest of Theseus.

The dog fell silent,
    the boys stood like statues
and one of them punted with a stick,
the waves shimmered nervously,
tadpoles swiftly
    flickered out of the wake,
the heavens
    stood still,
and the man stretched out his hand.

It was a hand
    reaching out across the ages,
it was a hand
    linking
    one world with another,
    life with death,
it was a hand
    joining everything together,
it caught the dog by the scruff of its neck

and then they sailed back
to the music of
an immense fanfare
of the dog's yapping.

It was not a question of that one dog.

It was not a question of that park.

Somehow it was a question
of our whole childhood,
    all of whose mischiefs
    will eventually out,
of all our loves,
of all the places we loved in
    and parted never to meet again,
of every prospect
    happy as grass,
unhappy as bone,
of every path up or down,

of every raft and all the other machines
we search for at our lathes
    and drawing-boards,

of everything we are reaching out for
round the corner of the landscape.

It was not an answer.

There are days when no answer is needed.

[GT]

The Czech lands are full of lions. We beat against the rails with lion's spirit,
said our poet. A double-tailed lion is in our national coat-of-arms. A cross-
eyed lion was on top of Pilsen's classic brewery. Even though in real life
we only have cats, some of them run over. But a lion is reassuring. [VR]

The zoo or about suffering

The zoo of the Iris Society was on the acacia-grown hillside above the Radbuza river. You got there by a track between wooden fences, behind which some suspicious characters resided, while the animals were just behind a bend in the path, in rusty cages. The most numerous were the racoons, at times totalling four, whereas the monkeys in a closed pavilion at the end of the path were busy waiting for their death sitting, each one alone, their black eyes fixed on the doors in expectation of some Uganda, Burundi or Uttar Pradesh. None of these came. Down below in the black river a water-sprite was drowning, blowing little bubbles from his green nose. The fat lady at the ticket window didn't look too well either, but she was selling white tickets which convinced us that we were still alive.

Dad always asked for a railwayman's discount, but in vain.

The zoo of the Iris Society was a place of small-scale suffering presented as entertainment. Since then we have all of us encountered a good many entertainments which were presented as soul-destroying suffering, but even more unseen suffering represented by a pair of familiar and visible monkeys' hands behind wire netting.

It was a good zoo. After all, it isn't so important what a lynx looks like as that it is here as a representative of two hundred and eighty thousand lynxes or lizards or earthworms or birds of paradise or primates who are likewise on their last legs, or more accurately, who are broken by death like prisoners interrogated under torture.

It was the best possible zoo because, without any technical fuss, it demonstrated the atmosphere of pain in which splendidly and heroically and randomly the fittest survive.

I have seen too many malignant tumours and tragic metabolical errors and severed spinal cords to exempt the human phenomenon from the sphere of the Iris Society's zoo.

Consent

Kress's dog caught a small cat
in the snow, bit its throat through
so it couldn't scream and remained
lying, opening and closing its little claws.

Then he took it in his teeth and dragged it a little further.

The cat hung there and looked.

It saw
a white cats' road beyond the horizon,
silver-gleaming with small ripples,
an ermine tunnel at the end of which
some god resembling a white mouse
was opening his front paws
and emitting a blinding radiance.

The cosy corner in the straw in the barn
was receding, mother
was watching like some white Nike
with black spots and the flight through the white weightless
tunnel was like the remotest mammalian consent
to the overcoming of improbability.

The small suspended cat doesn't want to return.

It consents.
More or less as a man would
in the cat's situation.

Butterflies

Yes, but what can you do against the flow of time? We're made from it, to repeat Jorge Luis Borges; it's a river that carries away, but we are that river, it's a tiger that destroys me, but I am that tiger; it's a fire that consumes, but I am that fire. The world, unfortunately, is real, I unfortunately am...I [fill in your name].

First I tried it with poems, but they had no colour.

Then I painted some kind of natural idylls with moss, a toadstool, a yellow flower and a gnome with a little red hat, but it lacked a third dimension.

I built little landscapes from little toy houses, little trees, castles and figures, but after a while they had to be cleared from the balcony area of the living room.

I collected and by chemical analysis, in the bathtub – which was used only on Saturdays, identified various rocks from the surroundings of Pilsen and stored them in drawers in the attic, neatly arranged in boxes, until Father put a stop to it because he was worried about the stability of the house.

But in the end I turned to butterflies. They were colourful, they were three-dimensional, they were real, they flew like mad, but they could be snatched from flight and dried on a limewood board in such a way that their mummies seemed more real than the ephemeral reality of the insects in flight. With the aid of a butterfly you could capture time in a green net and Lo, the Lord beheld it, and it was very good.

Never since have I developed such a perfect technology. I had several extensive illustrated books for the identification of butterflies and moths. I had a battery of limewood boards, called pinning boards. From the little jars of toothpaste (toothpaste in jars, according to Father, was much more economical than in tubes) I made stunning jars, with cotton-wool saturated with ammonia at the bottom. My collection grew in twenty-five boxes, black on top and white inside, with a peat base to take special entomological pins. Tiny little tags, labels with the name of the butterfly, the date and place of its capture and any circumstances deserving special mention. A powerful and safe fragrance of paradichlorbenzene. Small boxes with cotton-wool for the storage of freshly caught and murdered specimens.

All my catching and preserving technology was in a knapsack with internal partitions, hanging from my shoulder but freely rotatable about the main vertical axis of my body, as a result of which I nearly fell from the Lomnický Peak, the highest peak in the Tatra mountains, but, as you can see, didn't quite.

But all that was only the inventory.

Above it all was that immeasurable poetical beauty of sun-drenched mountain glades, where the swallow-tails had their air-fields, those noble Papilionidae which are the equals of Apollo and Mercury. The sacred groves of aspen, on whose cracked and sap-oozing boles Red Admirals and Camberwell Beauties, as nervous as they were delicate, would settle. The beechwoods, where some lappet moths and hawk moths, Aglaia tau of the Bombycoidea, would streak across like bullets at the execution of the Communards. The twilight after hot summer days, when hawk moths (Spingidae) attack phlox and goat's leaf like helicopter gunships. Naive Cabbage Whites and Cloudless Sulphurs (Pieridae) play over the meadows like a simple folksong of somewhat dim-witted goose girls who get pregnant even before harvest-home. Giant Peacocks (Saturniidae) which have to be raised from caterpillars or bought at Mr Frič's heavenly shop in Prague (now there's a fountain in its place, which either does not play or, if playing, throws up more dirt than water). And on frosty autumn evenings the Measuring Worm Moths (Oper-optera brumata) are the last argument of free flight against frost.

All the beauty of the world on metallically shimmering wings, more brittle than virginity and more mysterious than the curse of runes.

Unfortunately the world is real.

Unfortunately within ten years all my butterflies in their twenty-five boxes were eaten by museum carpet-beetles and other parasites which nurture a grudge against human immortality.

Unfortunately all that's left is the pins, the boxes and the labels.

And so I started writing poems again.

Poems aren't eaten by anything, except stupidity.

Boy catching butterflies

Only
a Painted Lady
and then he'll have
all the world's dust-like scales
preserved in boxes.

And so with a green key
he opens the undergrowth,
with a black key the forest,
with a blue key
the sky in the streams.

And so with questioning eyes
he opens
water, air, earth and fire,
all the way to love,
and so he opens
the summer's music and the winter's music,
all the way to the naked harmony
of the human heart.

With a wretched net over his shoulder
he wanders from tree to tree,
over equators and poles,
he hops and skips, and sees the sun,
walks on, and sees the moon,
limps on, and sees the earth,
stands still, and sees the end.

Grey hair,
grey dust-like scales.

He has a hundred Painted Ladies

And hardly seems
to see them.

That day we entered life

From outside the clear morning light was falling on the carpet and the patterns were purple and blue. The music stopped and a dark voice came on...From the early hours of today the German army has been occupying Bohemia and Moravia...What does it mean? grandmother called up from downstairs, but everybody was silent and it was as if a huge hand was covering the town, and the table, and the coffee, and the briefcase, and our eyes, and the washbasin, and the coats. And light snow was beginning to fall.

Down Klatovská drove a greenish-grey car with a German army WH plate, driving on the right. The Czech cars, used to driving on the left, found themselves going the other way. The trams found themselves going the other way. History was stepping into the street. The cars stopped and the tram sneaked along the walls. The car with the WH plate drove through victoriously, the helmets of angels flashing inside it. On the station platforms stood soldiers with bayonets fixed against those alighting. A few people had Czechoslovak tricolours on their lapels. The bayonets remained motionless. School was permitted.

Near Rolnická a dog had been run over. Tufts of black hair were rolling on the ground. The air was filled with a strange smell of aniseed.

School was permitted. We had Greek.

'...hé myri Achaiois alge ethéken, pollas d'ifthimous psychás Hádi proilapsen héroón, autous te helória teuche kynessin oiónoisi te pási, ...' Translate, said the Greek master, his voice was veiled and his face was all red. '...thousands of pains he inflicted on the Achaeans and many noble souls of heroes he flung into Hades and their bodies he left to the dogs and all kinds of birds...' His voice was veiled and his face was all red, the classroom was an isolated world of quiet and crackles and a single faint voice, but from above the huge hand of silence was closing. '...nouson ana straton órse kakén...he sent down a terrible sickness upon the camp...' Why do we still have Greek lessons, said something. Just because, said something. School ended at ten and we walked home. There was snow in the air and above the Škoda plant hung a black flag of smoke. We walked home round the familiar corners, over the old paving stones. We walked backwards.

That day we entered life. It was the fifteenth of March 1939.

Who'd have thought that we'd manage such an entry (into life) twice more.

We'll go up the tower

When you no longer get a B for singing
we'll go up the tower.
When you're bigger and there's no wind
we'll go up the tower.
When my heart doesn't trouble me
we'll go up the tower.

Meanwhile history swept over the land
like a mechanised rifle division,
from the gallery on top of the tower of St Bartholomew
the long, the short and the sharp-eyed would gaze
and suicides would jump
and the city would lick them clean
like a bitch its puppies,
leaving no spot.

From the tower you could see
the edge of the world. The Thirty Years' War,
St Nepomuk and a mendicant monk
on the path through the old barley fields.

But we didn't go up the tower.
We walked horizontally.
And when we did make up our minds
the tower was closed because the stairs were rotten.

So we got accustomed
to the quiet, phlegmy, woollen
endorphin life
of horizontal suicides.

To one on his back in the dark a voice tells of a past. With occasional
reference to the present and more rarely to a future, as for example:
'You'll end as you are now...' as it was written by Samuel Beckett. [VR]

The Germans

In Peták Square the Germans would get on the tram for Bory. They'd take their time over it, merely to show that this was a slave tram. The driver rang his bell and prepared to move off. The Germans began to howl in a Hunnish manner and an officer with black collar flashes adroitly jumped behind the vehicle and pulled the wheel off the trolley cable.

All the Germans then got on board in a leisurely manner and, quite politely really, called the driver a Czech pig.

Considering that the wheel on the trolley wire is something like the covenant between Abraham and the Lord of Hosts, we realised that we were eradicated from the Bible.

Then on one occasion, it was after dark, I was riding a little further in the open trailer No. 29, over the bridge and across the rail track of the southern suburb halt. By then there was only a small Hitlerjugend boy on the platform of the trailer. He stepped up to me and without a word tried to push me out of the car on to the receding pavement.

Surprisingly I was stronger.

I held out and then, on Chod Square, someone else got on.

It wasn't surprising that the boy should have done this. What was surprising was that he did it wordlessly, like a normal everyday duty.

For the next forty years in Chod Square I was always reminded of Rilke's words, *Wer spricht vom Siegen, Überstehen ist Alles.*

Herbarium

In our street stood maples in blossom
and quiet flowed like
maple syrup.

Two Gestapo men in leather coats
were leading Senator Winter, he was
lightly dressed, in a raincoat and
nervously jerked his head.

In the next street burst
the long pods of catalpas.
In our street stood maples in blossom
and quiet flowed like
maple syrup.

Two Czech STB men in leather coats
once more were leading Senator Winter, he was
again lightly dressed, in a raincoat and
nervously jerked his head.

In the next street dropped
the downy blossoms of plane-trees
like splinters of small fragmentation bombs.
In our street stood maples in blossom
and quiet flowed
like maple syrup.

Someone
had turned the street upside down,
so that Winter was led across a nervous sky,
while the leaves of maples, catalpas and plane-trees
are kept in our herbarium and we hope
that from them will burst
a singing song-bird.

The station

In the night raid on 17 April the station building received a direct hit and some German hospital trains were destroyed in the sidings. In the morning I only got as far as the square in front of the station which was submerged under the railway bridge and the two stone walls of the platforms. On the pavements along the walls several layers of corpses were already stacked up, some in uniform, in shirts, and without shirts.

Their faces were stony, red, white, grey and yellow.

Only death makes us multicoloured.

It was the greatest accumulation of people ever seen in front of Pilsen station.

It was like broad strips or bands of fields, well-ploughed. Up above, a lark seemed to be singing. But they were pin-headed Allied fighters.

It was in a deep hollow, but Goethe's *Over all hilltops is quiet* now applied here.

And in the collapsed guts of the main building was a shelter, where our railway medical teams assembled in an air raid. The shelter was probably never found. That night I was late getting to the station. I was late. Bombs had already begun to drop, and so I turned back home.

That's why I'm still able to quote Goethe.

Five minutes after the air raid

In Pilsen,
twenty-six Station Road,
she climbed to the third floor
up stairs which were all that was left
of the whole house,
she opened her door
full on to the sky,
stood gaping over the edge.

For this was the place
the world ended.

Then
she locked up carefully
lest someone steal
Sirius
or Aldebaran
from her kitchen,
went back downstairs
and settled herself
to wait
for the house to rise again
and for her husband to rise from the ashes
and for her children's hands and feet to be stuck back in place.

In the morning they found her
still as stone,
sparrows pecking her hands.

[GT]

Here we are above Nádražní Street, where five minutes after the raid that lady was looking for her third floor, which had been blown away. To commemorate the event the trolley buses now run from the Central Station to the Central Cemetery and back again. [FD]

Manon

That raid also put paid to a house on Fügnerová street, where my classmate Spíšek lived, with whom I had a very positive relationship so that I actually lent him my copy of Nezval's *Manon*. After the bomb all that was left of the house was one load-bearing wall with bits of the different floors, like little shelves for parrots. On the first floor, at the Spíšeks, that shelf still held a bedside table and on it my *Manon*, with Mrs Burešová's picture downward, so that the débris only scratched the back cover.

Since then these scratches have somehow healed, they are now hardly visible.

Maybe that's what is meant by *Omnia vincit amor*.

Or by an optical illusion of memory.

The parallel syndrome

Two parallels
always meet
when we draw them by our own hand.

The question is only
whether in front of us
or behind us.

Whether that train in the distance
is coming
or going.

Bombs

For my railway training in so-called commercial service, like selling tickets, I was attached to Valcha station. When there was a raid on I would carry the station-master's gas mask and fireman's helmet to the shelter in the cutting, which had originally been a sewer. I don't know what he carried, probably a list of closely watched trains. From the shelter, apart from the stationmaster and his moustache, we would peep out during the raids to see what was dropping where.

We saw the silvery American bombers and below them something like golden commas, full stops and dashes, which would fly for a while and then, bronze-coloured, turn downwards. The dashes turned into roaring distant explosions and the yellow living quarters of the warders of Bory penitentiary rose rather ridiculously into the air, all in a piece, and dropped back again like a bride on a vampire's wedding night. All was concealed then in a cloud of dust and non-dust.

The ground shook and the stationmaster's moustache had an unearthly look in the half-light of the sewer, like some dark northern lights on a grand gloved ball. At the exit from the sewer wild thyme and chickweed flowered. On the blue inflorescence sat a female meadow-blue which, regardless of its name, was of brown colour and elegantly stuck out its slim abdomen. The tremor and distant roar, the northern light and the airborne penitentiary meant nothing to this grouping.

Noise is the school of silence and death is the basic practice text of what is called life.

To this day I see in the sky over the southern edge of Pilsen those golden dashes and the daylight aurora borealis in the moustache of some present or past foul-mouthed bastard.

And that brown meadow-blue is still sitting on the wild thyme. Its name is Helena.

The bomb

Murder in the lithosphere.
Clay burst from the rock,
fire flowed from the clay.

At the base of the crater
a naked, tender, loving
frog's heart
still beats.

Identity

The principal contribution to a Pilsen identity is not so much ancient history as recent events. Pilsen is famous mainly through having been liberated in 1945 by General Patton's army, whereas the rest of Czechoslovakia owed a joyful debt of gratitude to Red liberation. Throughout the forty years of dictatorship of the proletariat this piece of history was more or less hushed up, but now it is notched up to Pilsen's identity as a great plus.

It is a kind of identity through contrast and difference, rather as if a caterpillar encountered an earth-worm and thereby realised that it had little feet underneath.

As a result I am more and more from Pilsen.

A significant step along those lines occurred near the little town of Columbus, Wisconsin. There are fourteen Columbuses in the United States, without any detriment to local civic pride or identity, which probably don't stem from the name. Near Columbus, Wisconsin, the landscape is wintery; in some American states it's somehow always winter, especially in Minnesota and Wisconsin. Along the road were frozen lakes and the frequent farms suggested that the region would be flowing with milk and honey if it wasn't so cold. Instead, the milk and honey was to be found inside the small and not-so-small cheese-dairies. There it was as warm as in a stable and as smelly as a Pilsen yeast factory – oh no, not quite, in that kind of stench no one in America would work, it was more like the anteroom of the manager of a Pilsen yeast factory. On the shelves huge rounds of Edam, Cheddar and Liederkranz were maturing and in silver-foamed metal tubs two workmen were mixing a yellow dough which to me looked already so homogeneous that back home they'd shrug and leave it at that. They were mixing even though it was a day of rest and they talked over their mixing paddles without looking up.

We'll learn to work like that when we've had some ten years of private-enterprise cheese-making.

Meanwhile we've got that freedom of ours which those Wisconsin cheese-makers never even dreamt of.

Where was I from, one of the cheese-makers asked. He was short and sinewy from his heel up to his paddle, with a high forehead.

I admitted that I was from Czechoslovakia – today this would need a longer explanation – but he also wanted to know the town.

Pilsen, I said with local loyalty. Pilsen.

'Ah, Pilsen,' he said in his American voice. 'Sure, that's where I bought it in my leg at the end of the war.' And he put down his paddle and shook my hand in token of historical and geographical harmony.

'Where?' I asked.

'There was some church and some kind of a theatre,' he said.

At this the mist and smog of time-past lifted and instinctively (I get an instinct every eight years) I saw that I had seen it.

It was on sixth May 1945, in the morning. The Sixty-third and Third divisions were entering the city in the face of slight opposition and we hastened to welcome them and wave little flags, or perhaps even lend an armed hand to the good deed. Over the local radio Mister Schindler was calling for help from Štrunc Park and some small-arms fire was heard from the Thirty-five Barracks and from Wilson Bridge. I had just got to the Municipal Theatre when some American armoured troop carriers appeared, with infantry advancing behind them. At the crossroads in front of the theatre firing suddenly broke out, as if glasses were falling out of a cupboard. The infantrymen took cover and fired at the little tower on top of the church, now the Czechoslovak Hussite church, from where little puffs appeared and bits of masonry dropped down, then a tank rolled up and fired a few rounds from its cannon and that was the end of resistance, except that the Czechoslovak Hussite church afterwards had some major maintenance costs; but before it all calmed down one of the infantrymen behind the carrier suddenly caught his leg, dropped his submachine-gun and writhed on the ground. After a while some US soldiers with an ambulance appeared and loaded the soldier with his leg. Somehow this seemed a good deal smoother than the way we deal with a road accident today and we were watching it all from the doorway to the buffet in the Adria building, believing that the plate glass would protect us.

Well, that writhing soldier in front of the Pilsen theatre was my cheesemaker in Wisconsin.

I have written about it in my American book *Angel on Wheels*, but only wistfully; in 1963 having been liberated by the US Army was like being HIV positive.

This then was a moment when I realised that to meet an American whom an SS sniper had hit in the leg outside the Adria building in Pilsen, and to meet him on a farm in Wisconsin, one of ten thousand similar farms, was in the category of immaculate conception. That it simply didn't agree with real-life probability, that it didn't agree at all was therefore very much OK because, according to

Stanislaw J. Lec, 'If everything has to agree, there's something wrong'.

So that 'actually coming from somewhere' is something unique and inalienable, it is another life that's growing inside us, yielding magical fruit, like Cinderella's hazelnuts.

If I'd come from the Moravian border (like that pretend Jeník Horák, alias Mícha in *The Bartered Bride*) or from some other place, I'd never have met my shot cheese-maker from Columbus, Wisconsin. My life would have run with a slight detour, a few minutes west or east, a detour at first insignificant but eventually, in the manner of a transverse, leading somewhere else. Not to come from Pilsen would have been like Hector not being from Troy or Ulysses from Ithaca, so that Telemachus wouldn't be his son and therefore in all probability wouldn't have set out for the Peloponnesus to seek news of his dad, so that he wouldn't have met Nestor, Menelaus or Helen, and his dad Ulysses would have fallen prey to Polyphemus and Athene wouldn't have helped him, and in the end Penelope wouldn't have remained faithful to him but would have succumbed to her wicked suitors, and without a happy ending Ulysses would not have been worth an epic and without the epic Homer wouldn't have been worth inclusion even in a penny dreadful. These then are the historical consequences if someone isn't actually from somewhere. In my own petty dimension of time such a deviation in my place of birth might have meant no more than a different surveillance man under the Bolsheviks, another direction of my nose when I broke it playing football in Štrunc Park, a less incompetent director of immunology in our institute and an impairment of the significance of Jiří Orten's *Ninth Elegy*. A few changes in beloved names and in the softness of touched hair.

I can't say that I am glad or proud to come from Pilsen. I just am from Pilsen and I bear this fact with full understanding. And if Pilsen were a town of some Islamic Jumhuriyah I'd feel nudged by fate to find at least some good hair on Allah and his imams, and if Pilsen had fallen into the hands of Hasidim I'd feel a theoretical urge to walk about in a long black coat and a white shirt buttoned up to the chin, with a broad-rimmed black hat from Nový Jičín pushed to the back of my head, with a full beard, sideburns and boots one size too big, so that, again in theory, I'd look as if the Lord had been chasing me ever since Yom Kippur, from the time of the October rains, with me having no time to change even in the heat of summer, in fact I'd try to look at least like black wool on a white lamb if Pilsen were under Hasidic rule.

Fortunately Pilsen has remained in the hands of the Pilseners, who are so inconspicuous and neutral as annelid worms in the land of Canaan.

The fall of Troy

From burning Troy we rescued
our wretched rags,
teeth in a water-glass
and our tattooed grandfather.

A short way down the ancient
quails were nesting again
and silver pikes were brushing
against a calm sky.

Some soldier,
pinned to the ground with a spear,
gave us a little wave.
Wormwood remained silent to us
and so was fumitory.

Just like home, grandfather said.

The bleating of lambs
vaulted our roof for us
over our heads.
The earth oozed manna.
Since the Precambrian rocks
nothing really happened.

And like an ingrown nail
digging into the flesh
our truth
was always with us

We slept in embrace,
our rags around us,
teeth in the water-glass.
Just like home, grandfather said.
Nothing in fact happened.
Except that we realised
that Troy
            had probably
                        really
fallen.

How the beast of war lay down

The day after the end of hostilities American soldiers were playing baseball in the streets of Pilsen.

The train from Prague then had to make a détour via Rudná and Rakovník. At Rudná in the fields we ran over a cow. The wheels screeched, damaged by the bones and two carriages began to jerk. We had hardly come to a halt when several platoons of rather grimy Soviet soldiers appeared and pulled the remains of the cow clear. Even before one managed to unhitch the carriages the cow had been carved up by bayonets alongside the track and a fire was being lit under a cauldron.

Just outside Rakovník in a sparse wood the railway track crossed a road. The barriers were down at the crossing, yet an approaching Russian jeep didn't even slow down but drove under the bars just in front of the engine. On the raised back seat a little green soldier had been sitting upright before the level crossing, but the barrier caught his head and flung him back. He lay on the sandy road surface, his heels jerking a little. The jeep on the other side didn't stop but disappeared in the woods.

When we got to Pilsen in the late afternoon the Americans were still pitching and catching with a leathery smack.

It turned out that the beast of war was lying down in two entirely different ways.

Place the Venus de Milo's head in her hands...wrote Jaroslav Seifert. The Pilsen tram hastened towards the same lyrical destination. [FD]

Interferon

Always just one demon in the attic.
Always just one death in the village. And the dogs
howling in that direction. And from the other end
the new-born child arrives, the only one
to fill the empty space in that wide air.

Likewise also cells infected by a virus
send out a signal all around them and defences
are mobilised so that no other virus
has any hope just then of taking root
or changing fate. This phenomenon
is known as interference.

And when a poet dies in the depth of night
a single black bird wakens in the thicket
and sings for all it is worth
while from the sky a black rain trickles down
like sperm or something,
the song is spattered and the choking bird
sings sitting on an empty rib-cage
in which an imaginary heart
awakes to its forever interfering
futility. And in the morning the sky is clear,
the bird is weary and the soil is fertilised.
The poet is no more.

In Klatovská Street, in Pilsen,
by the railway bridge, there was
a shop with quilted bedcovers.
In times when there's a greater need
for a steel cover over our continent
business in quilted bedcovers
is slack. The shopkeeper was hard up.
Practical men when hard up usually
turn to art.
In his shopwindow, open to the interior
of his shop, its owner built
a gingerbread house of quilts
and every evening staged

a performance about a quilted
gingerbread house and a red-quilted
Little Red Riding Hood, while his wife
in this quilted masquerade was alternately
the wolf or the witch, and he himself
a padded-out Hansel,
or Gretel, Red Riding Hood or grandmother.
The sight of the two old people
crawling about in swollen billows
of textiles round the chubby cottage
was not unambiguous. It was a little like
the life of sea cucumbers in the mud
under a reef. Outside thundered
the approaching surf of war and they
conducted their quilted
pantomime outside time and action.

For a while children would stand outside but
soon they would go home. Nothing was sold.
But it was the only pantomime
at that time. The black bird sang
and rain poured into a rib-cage
wearing the Star of David.

But in the actors under those quilted covers
l'anima allegra must have just then awoken
and so, sweating and rapt, they acted
their undersea *commedia dell'arte*,
thinking there was a backstage until
a scene was finished, jerkily they moved
from shopwindow to gingerbread house and back,
with the exuberance of Columbines
stricken by polio, while the music
of fifes and drums did not reach them.

Or else they thought that such a deep
humiliation of the customary dignity of age
interfered with the steps of gentlemen
in leather coats and with
the departure of trains to human slaughterhouses.
It did.

The black bird sang and the ruined
sclerotic hearts leapt in their breasts,
and then one morning when they didn't play
and had not even raised the blind –
the sky was clear, the soil was fertilised –
the quilted bedcovers were confiscated
for the eastern front and the actors
transferred to the backstage
of the world, called Bergen-Belsen.
No trace is left of the shop today:
it's now a greengrocer's with woody parsnips.

Always just one death in the village.
Always just one demon.
Great is the power of the theatre, even if
it always does get knocked down in the end
and flung backstage.

The dogs howl in that direction.
And the butterfly pursues the man
who stole the flowers.

When we did autopsies at the psychiatric
hospital in Bohnice, filled with the
urban exudations of relative futility,
the car would tip us out amidst the ward blocks
whose inmates waved from windows
with some kind of May Day pennants, and then
one went, hugely alone,
beyond a spinney to the solitary morgue, where
the naked bodies of ancient schizophrenics
awaited us, along with two live inmates; one of them
would pull the corpses up from underground
with a rope hoist and place them
upon the tables as a mother might an infant
for baptism, while the other was lurking, pen ready poised,
in a dark corner to write up
the Latin protocol, and he wrote faultlessly.
Neither of them uttered the slightest sound, only
the hoist shaft moaned…and the knife
drawn over skin and dermis made a sound
of satin tearing…and they were always

enormous and unprecedented pneumonias
and tumours as big as dragons' eggs,
it rained into the opened thorax –
and in that roaring silence one had to
break the line of an angel's fall
and dictate the logical verdict
on a long-sentenced demon...
and the schizophrenic's pen in the corner
busily scraped across the paper
like an eager mouse.

We need no prompters
said the puppets haughtily.

The air of that anatomical theatre
was filled with interferon,
it was a great personal demonstration
against malignant growth, it was
a general amnesty for the walls, entropy
was abjured for the moment

because there are no bubbles at the bottom
to burst under the breeze.

The red balloon outside rose up
to an unsuspected sky, its chains
strained by the certainty that the nearer the inferno
the greater the paradise,
the nearer the prison cell
the greater the freedom.
Cantabit vacuus coram latrone viator.

And that is the weird essence of the theatre
that an actor stripped of everything mounts to
the very top of the conflagration
and everything else dies down, falls silent
like a long-hunted animal, its muscles
still twitching but with endorphines
and an infinite peace in the brain.

Yes, even a whale will sometimes leave the school,
hurl itself into shallow water and perish in the sun

like a levelled cathedral, with pushed-out penis,
and death is instantly buried
in a grain of sand
and the sea laughs.

Go ask the tree-stumps; in broken language
they preach about saplings. And in the jargon
of galactic white dwarfs the stars
of the main sequence shine forever.

In the non-Euclidean curved space,
which eludes understanding as much as
the interference of the theatre,
you ceaselessly hear the voices of children
from the primary school of death,
children from the puppet tragedies of the kitchen
and children from the junketings of war,
when skewering them on lances
with their wriggling little legs
provided spice like curry for the mercenaries,
voices of children eluding understanding –

But we've washed behind our ears,
we've stopped pulling the cat's tail,
we've stopped shoving our fingers
into electric sockets –

What else is there left in the universe
of hominisation, slow as the decay of tritium,
than the doctrine of the growing sense of shame of demons:
since Aztec times high priests no longer
offer up sacrifice while dressed in the skin
of a freshly flayed prisoner.

We need no prompters, they said –

Once on St Nicholas' Day, the man acting the Devil,
dead drunk, fell down some stairs and lay there,
and a child, experiencing that embarrassing
joy mere inches from terror,
ran out after the thump and called:

Mummy, come here, there's a dead devil –

And so he was, even though the actor
picked himself up after another tot. Maybe the dogs howled,
but only by a black mistake.
In the sky shone the stars of the main sequence,
the bird was getting ready in the thicket,
the child shivered a little
from the chill of three million years,
in that wide air, but
they prompted him, poetically,

you're only imagining all this,
look, the butterfly's already
bringing the flowers back...and
there's no other devil left...and
the nearer paradise...

He believed, and yet he didn't.

The fraction line

The poorly ventilated spaces of the Czechoslovak State Grammar School on the corner of Husova and Škodova street were enlivened chiefly by Theseus, Ovid, the caretaker Nocar, Helen of Troy, Charles Darwin and the god Ares who, outside the building from the sixth form up, wore a greyish-green uniform, a pot-shaped helmet and smelly shaft-boots.

My hero was chiefly our Greek master, a one-armed Patrocles called Müller, in whose working-class Prague diction the philosophy of the Hylozoists sounded like a topical problem, and along with him Antonín Špelda, a cunning mathematical-physical Ulysses. Špelda taught us one vital step which, in my opinion, is the very foundation of cities, townhalls, parliaments, state visits, private visits, poems, discussions, science, interaction with a computer, economic budgets and love letters. Seeing our painful embarrassment over the third power of 1 minus 3 a^2 divided by 1 minus a^2, Špelda, his head buried deep behind his desk – and the depth of burial was proportionate to the depth of his exasperation with the stupidity of the world – would grunt: Make a fraction line. Don't dither. Simply say: we'll make a fraction line. After that you'll manage somehow.

If I ever had As or Bs it was because I always first made a fraction line, moreover without dithering.

Whenever nowadays we walk past the dark grey corner building of our first *alma mater*, walking calmly where before eight in the morning we invariably raced like fleet-footed Achilleses or scared rabbits, we sometimes remember the fraction line.

Whenever we sit, or even stand, before the task of facing the recurrent stupidity and persistent sadness of the world we always remember. And make a fraction line.

The day of the Pollyanna

That day the dough didn't rise.
The clock stopped in the kitchen.
Against all hope
the tram again turned round at its final stop
at Slovany.

But in the second car,
right at the back sat a small girl
in a big blue cap,
she held a doll
looking like a three-months-old foetus of a tapir
and in a small antimony voice she sang –

Don't cry... don't cry... don't cry.

Even though nobody felt like crying,
least of all the tapirs.

On the phenomenon of the family zither

In defiance of Miroslav Horníček's theory that mankind is diminishing in number because every individual has two grandfathers and four great-grandfathers our family was simpler – I had one grandfather and one grandmother because Father's father married Mother's mother on 3 September 1907 after both had been widowed.

On the other hand, the members of this thus simplified family had some staying power, for none of them died before their ninetieth year of earthly life, having developed some slight senile dementia, so that in the end Grandmother didn't know if she was in Pilsen or Josefov, and Mother made the confusion worse by mixing Spičák and Prague. For Grandmother, moreover, in defiance of Horníček's theory, her son, i.e. Father, split into two separate individuals; thus when he wore his black nutria fur-coat and came home in it, Grandmother would try to take it from him, saying that he'd stolen it from Joe, so that Father had to beat a hasty retreat and come in a second time, when he was recognised as Joe and could keep his coat.

The war didn't bother Grandmother too much because she believed that Josefov was strongly fortified; instead she would sometimes look at the stove and say: Did you see him? Over there! – See whom, we'd ask. – The devil, of course, she'd say. But he's hiding now.

Moreover, the pendulum clock would be stopped in our household, so it could have a rest, and the electricity turned off, so it shouldn't unnecessarily leak from the sockets.

Unfortunately our simplified family was not lucky enough to attain the philosophical heights of James Thurber's family who, in reply to the police, summoned in the middle of the night and searching for the cause of the alarm and asking: What's this here?, said: This is the zither where our guinea-pig used to sleep.

But we tried.

Besides, I used to have a zither as a little boy, and later also a guinea-pig, but it escaped to our neighbours and someone ate it.

Pietà

Flowers
   they're always immediately put in a vase,
the vase in the hall, in the cool, in the dark,
so the flowers should last longer.

They died.
   Their little urns stand
in the hall, in the cool, in the dark
and a blind spider
looks after them to make sure –

Otherwise it would all be
too sad.

The horses

Before, at the corner of Czech Legionaries Street and Smetana Park, opposite the Theatre, the building of the Riunione Adriatica went up, on whose ground floor the Adria buffet was lately installed, reminiscent of Dalskabáty, the sinful village of Jan Drda's novel, including its half-forgotten long-serving devils, and where I stood before its locked doors when the Americans arrived; well then, at that corner, in my grey childhood, which evidently reaches back into Metternich's times, there used to stand a green post-office building. At its corner a magic lamp-lighter used to light a gas lamp with an absurd bamboo pole, and in its basement were the stables of the post horses, which, when taken out, drew blue boxes on red wheels, which were the postal carts containing postal packages, and which, when not taken out, emitted a horsey smell of hay, hair and horse-droppings, a smell equalled only by the smell of a bakery. All children's Sunday matinees, the King – Mr Rabas, the Queen – Mrs Rabas, Punch – Miss Šárková, the Sorcerer – Mr Zavrel, who in the opera wore skiing socks and sonorously represented also Lutobor or Vladislav or Přemysl, all performances bore for me the signature of that equine smell.

Because on this spot the Riunione Adriatica building subsequently rose, and the Adria buffet with its forgotten half-drunken devils, and an American infantry troop carrier, which admittedly had to go underground for the next 44 years, and because across the road the Theatre now towered not only with Messrs Zavřel but also with Messrs Horníček and Hofbauer and Pistorius, there are so many historical layers here that I regard it as out of the question that the post horses should no longer exist. They simply belong to the substratum.

Especially when, a little way across the next street, Huss Street or Lenin Street, or whatever it is today, there was the Brown House and after it, naturally, the Red House, or for students and other wayfarers the House of Miracles or the Haunted Castle, where dedicated skeletons, henchmen and mercenaries held sway, who by their very existence above ground demanded something fundamental below it, rather like the Ace of Acorns, known as the swine, has under its feet the city's coat-of-arms or the Eight of Balls has under it a tethered prancing bay with red reins.

The Pilsen post horses were quite simply conserved by the diluvium and alluvium and, unseen, continue to live beneath the town, smelling in their brewing-charter cellars and drawing their blue postal boxes with packages for Wenceslas II, Henry the Founder, the first judge of the city, to Bavůrek of Švamberk, the enemy and malefactor of the city, who was spontaneously executed in the Main Square, which was one of the truly original local performances at the beginning of the sixteenth century, as well as to Mansfeld, Tyl and Škoda; these horses neigh mutedly beneath the city and in our more modest circumstances are what in Babylon ran between the E-temen-an-ki zigurat, the Esagila and the Ezida.

I simply demand horses beneath my native city.

I don't demand the worship of Marduk, the principal Babylonian god.

I don't demand the worship of the horse, even though the horse's eye is worthy of worship if you are acquainted with Shaffer's play *Equus*.

I merely demand that we should believe in the horses beneath the city, seeing that we believe in such a lot of nonsense anyway.

A postal horse with a blue postal van. In those ancient days the horses still grew wings and the postmen used the paternoster lift to ride up to the first heaven, where the god Hermes checked if the mail was correctly franked. [VR]

The searching tram

Trams are forever running
round and round, searching
among the flashing of the granite cobbles
for the blind track of the philosophers.

The track of liberation
from flashing. The track
Abide awhile
you are so fair.
All round
will stand
Atlases,
Stone Guests,
menhirs,
dolmens,
stalagmites and stalactites.

Stone faces
from Easter Island,
all liberated
from the flashing of blood corpuscles
and oxidative phosphorylisation
in the cells of the brain stem.

Here the trams will be
perpetuated to the singing of choirs
of angels, succubuses and incubuses
and become arks
of the New Covenant

between the deaf-and-dumb
and granite
with a short half-life of decay.

The fowl

Above the city towers a metaphysical hen's head with its dull dark eye fixed on eternity. It opens its beak, but its cackling is heard below, where its triple scaly claws are frantically scratching about in the ashes. Its ovaries in the town's cellars are swollen because even metaphysics must propagate.

When the chicken's head is chopped off on the block behind the house, by the granite foundation wall and under the overgrown pear-tree, its body shoots off like grapeshot from a Prussian cannon. Drops of blood are scattered over the ageing sand and the rejuvenated Timothy grass.

It is a fowl of stupidity.

For reason ends with each of us in motionless rigidity, on a urine-rusted wire-mattress bed, with vomit in the corners of the mouth. In a track-suit, because we were just about to get up. Except that Yelena Alexandrovna didn't notice that we were already dead. On the parquet floor a big Brockhaus of dust was swirling.

At the moment of exit a muted crowing is heard, in the cellar the oviduct is working and white, and the bloody feathery body beats outside the window.

The whole problem is that hens are somewhat immortal and continue to multiply, using vermicular Latin which has altogether only four words.

Again and again the trampling of rhinoceroses is heard in the streets and the smacking of the soles of dromedaries.

The whole problem is that stupidity multiplies in a herd, whereas reason is divided by the number of heads, and reason thus diminishes with multitude.

If a herd of Diderots were trampling in the street it wouldn't sound all that different.

The hen's head over the city is in fact a hundred-member committee which has just announced that everything will be done to ensure that all citizens arrive at mummification in good health.

Anatomy of January

On the metacarpals
the carpals
with desiccating cartilages,
the ulna as
a ruler for parrots.

A thread fastened to the joint,
stretching, leading beyond the horizon
to the southwest.

And ravens fall from the sky
under oath.

The city under the ground

All that remains of a city buried by no matter who for three hundred to three thousand years is a hill, mostly a grass-grown one. When on Khalkidhike we followed the signposts to its ancient capital city of Olynthos, famous for its regular blocks, sewerage, baths and jewellery, as well as for being frequently liberated from the yoke of another and therefore illegitimate ruler, we found a wire fence. *No Entry* in Greek, a lilac hawk moth, two Greek tortoises, the dry stony bed of a stream, and beyond the fence nothing but a hill with steep flanks.

No one had dug it over yet, or even properly looted it.

The tendency of cities to form hills overgrown with scrub and xerophile grasses is something instinctive and primal, something like the tendency of a dog to curl up into a ball before turning to sleep and turn right over. Or the tendency of a sleeping child to pull the blanket over its head.

That's why the pickaxe is an essential tool of archaeology. Our dreams do not float in the air, our dreams are preserved in the ground like fermenting gherkins in brine. Our dreams do not rise higher and higher. With the passage of time our dreams sink into the lithosphere, so that the difference between what is buried and what is historically missing is merely the lid over the burial chamber.

The cities which did not pull a blanket of scrub over themselves are those which were covered by other cities, so that we walk over heads and stand on altars and other instruments of thanksgiving for still being able to give thanks.

Besides, it's somehow safer underground. I have never heard of anyone depositing the gross national or the net personal product in a ziggurat or a donjon, the kind of round tower in which, in Ireland and elsewhere in Europe (but it was the Celts who were particularly fond of it) at the time of an invasion the whole village installed itself, pulled up the ladder and at the top of the viewing tower waited to see who would hold out longer. Every careful citizen always buried his treasure.

That is the basic prerequisite of life in human society – to bury what can be buried, like an opossum its plundered eggs, a squirrel its nuts, and a dog its bone. Which is why we sometimes find ourselves under the earth even before we croak and even before our city is, either in the name of historical justice or through tectonic activity, razed to the ground.

This postulate has the status of an axiom.

Thus in our garden on Mánesova Street my father, as I still remember, buried an earthenware pot with some Austro-Hungarian valuables. An officer's pistol from the first war, which he'd once shown me while my mother was all the time pressing me to her bosom, afraid the pistol might go off and the bullet describe a 180° arc around the bedroom. A Cossack sabre from the film *Cavalry Patrol*, which some careless extra had lost in the snow at the Godlhof on Spičák mountain. I was very proud of it, but father regarded it as a risky object during the Nazi Protectorate period. An American pistol from May 1945, of which I was very proud but which father regarded as risky at the time of the final liberation of the working people of town and country by the heroic KGB. Two American incendiary bombs, big hexagonal or octagonal things which we found in our attic on 25 April 1945. Even they had become somehow illegal after the February Victory of redemption. The leather case of a Rollei-flex, because for one thing it stank and for another it was too much the wrong kind of thing. Some piece or other of jewellery in a polythene bag because of the persecution of the bourgeoisie. Documents showing that grandmother had a haberdashery shop, also in polythene. A few cut-glass vases. A picture of Eduard Beneš and T.G. Masaryk on horseback. And who knows what else. Today we'd have to bury Karl Marx's *Das Kapital* if we'd had it. And who knows what else.

That precisely is the axiom that it's better to have things in the ground than above ground.

I believe that our neighbours the Noseks buried their wheelbarrow which was of excess value for their plot of land.

Burying is a midnight activity, secret and careful. That's why next morning we don't know its exact location. And after a year we only know approximately under which flower bed. And after ten years we only know approximately in which garden. And after twenty years we have no idea that we buried anything at all or the whereabouts of the pickaxe in question.

Thus arises a pickaxe relay between persons and metapersons, between the substrates of history and the uncoverers of history. There also arises a kind of permanent symbiosis between the performance of life and the performance of archaeology.

On the city principle I regard as the most enchanting the interconnection between life and metalife, between civic striving and archaeological ease.

I am glad that our family made a material contribution to that process.

The old people's garden

Malignant growth of ivy.
And unkempt grass,
because it no longer matters.
Beneath the trees an invasion
of fruitful Gothic.
Dusk had fallen, mythological
and toothless.

But the Minotaur beat it
through a hole in the fence.
The Icaruses were caught
somewhere in spiders' webs.

In the dawn's early light
the disrespectfully grey, insolent
frontal bone of fact
is revealed.
And it yawns without word.

Bridges, footbridges and souls

The iron footbridge in Pilsen, known as the Prague Bridge, suspended from the railway bridge over the Radbuza river like a liana bridge for hanuman monkeys, was, and still is, so narrow that during the passage of a slightly above-normal citizen it was necessary to turn, or even to retreat, to the little passing balcony from the angle-iron rail and wire netting. Even in poor visibility it was possible to predict the approach of an above-normal citizen by the tomtoms on the wooden floor of the little bridge, which such a citizen would make swell up to the intensity of the tympani in Beethoven's Fifth Symphony.

For a young lad within the norm this is a footbridge of choice, for here he will realise that his dimensions are in fact ideal, whereas the sexually mature adults, who incidentally engage in immoral acts beneath the vaulting of the railway bridge, do not have such suitable parameters either coming or going. Likewise any wheeled vehicle except a child's scooter causes a disturbance here, and I can remember the splendid quarrel between two citizens, one of whom was pushing a wheelbarrow and argued, against the inconvenienced complainant going the other way, that he was from the railway and had a card proving his entitlement to a privilege ticket and to concessionary coal. No one can blame us boys within the norm if we tended towards surrealism even while still in Pilsen.

This friendly miracle of engineering suspended under the sky above the mirror-like surface of the Radbuza, which was only occasionally disturbed by excrement or a Moses basket, was in fundamental contrast to the short fat Wilson Bridge, which was, and is, made of granite, regularly spanning the roaring weir and the mutedly humming power station, and across which even very large motorcars would run, complete with drivers. Wilson Bridge, I used to think, was the granite masterpiece of some Wilson or other who completed his achievement by the two kiosks at the beginning and the end of it, so that he might sell green algae there, or that he himself lay down across the river roaring at the weir and then turned to stone.

Admittedly not in the slapdash way as the man in the story by Franz Kafka, spanning the abyss and forming a bridge which collapsed with pain under the first gentleman crossing it in a bowler hat and with a sharp-tipped umbrella.

The immense merit of bridges which lead from somewhere to

111

somewhere else and thus escape the circular essence of the native nest was most joyously obvious on Saxon Bridge, which was blessed by St Bonaventure, St Jude Thaddeus, the Holy Cross, St Francis, St John Nepomuk, St Roch and John Saskander, even though it led over the Mže river only for a short section of its length and for a long stretch over the poor Roudná and Rychtářka neighbourhoods and over the rather gloomy council school. Their blessing was exceedingly welcome, given the boredom of crossing such a small and sorrowful water. As a matter of fact it seemed that at the merest pretext a surge of high water would race down from Kozolupy and engulf the low bridge. So that we would have a bridge under the river and a river over the bridge and St Juda Thaddeus along with St Roch would be paddling in the shallow brown waters like wapiti elks. Tankards would be floating out from the Bohemian Lion public house and in the Rychtárka neighbourhood, on the leaky roof of a disintegrating house, Marie Rehbergerová would stand in her only dark-blue party dress and with such a strange smile as that when I once took her to a dance lesson and my classmates Hrádek and Benda shouted at me: *Holub, where d'you think you're dragging that coffin?*

And below Bory, on the road to Litice, across the valley which was known in our family as Slav Valley but, so they say, is actually Czech, there is on a sharp bend a small stone bridge on which anyone riding a bike even in the La Tene period, was bound to come to grief and any number of bell-shaped beakers were broken before the simple-minded Slavs arrived on the scene and preferred to wade across.

The footbridges and bridges of Pilsen lead from somewhere to somewhere else, but basically you're always here, which must have pleased Jan Kajetán Tyl, the author of our national anthem.

And I believe that a bridge is the closest approach to the soul of a city and to the natural disposition of a city and to the natural position of a city, so that you best get the feeling of New York if you cross the cosmic magnitude of the Verrazano Bridge in daytime and the super-Christmassy illuminations of Washington Bridge at night, not to mention the infernal Manhattan Bridge or Brooklyn Bridge, that San Francisco is defined by the suicidally exalted Golden Gate Bridge, that London is as stately as Tower Bridge including all those halberds, and that Paris is most itself under the Pont Mirabeau, where the Seine rolls its quiet waves and all we've loved, all our loves.

Švanda the Bagpiper went into the world over the bridges of

Pilsen. And he does that all the time, because whenever he steps over a straying root or he's left his bagpipes behind he has to go back for them. Or while passing someone on the iron footbridge he tore a hole in his goatskin bag and had to go somewhere else to stick it together again.

The subconscious of a city are its underground passages and cellars. Pilsen has a 25-kilometre-long subconscious, and quite apart from Freud this was a damned useful thing during air raids. [VS]

The map of Europe

The dusty road
leads through undergrowth to
dry field paths, where
campion, ragged robin and chickweed flourish.

The stones chant
between their teeth, for no machine-guns
are heard.

Behind the hill the village recovers
with red and grey roofs
after its anaphylactic shock
when the same thing had
happened too often.

It's still Saturday after the war.
My father, rucksack on back
like an impoverished marsupial,
pushes his bike uphill,
because beyond the horizon
he'll get black-market eggs
and milk for his can.

Father's motion is virtual.
In reality
it's the landscape, the stones, the campions,
the village and the nut-tree that fall behind.

The same is true of the position
of the observer.

As long as I'm here, therefore,
Father will push his bike uphill
where the track bends,

as a sensitive static spot on the moving,
inert, dissolving map of Europe.

Darkness

So after two years in New York I arrived back in Europe in 1967 on board the SS *Franconia*, Cunard Line. Unloading in Liverpool was a very un-American pig's breakfast. Negotiation with a tough and blimpish British official about the loading of the miserable remains of my luggage in London was not a feast for the spirit and was very unlike the swift and basically tolerant customs of America. Europe is a bit of a shock when you've crossed the Atlantic.

Prague was like a small town in Tsarist Russia, where you can't tell Chlestyakov from patriarch, if only because of the universal murk and swamp which so readily deters cars and the *dramatis personae*.

In Pilsen it was evening and there was – for an eye used to America – darkness as when a whale swallows not only the sun and the moon but also the enlightenment. It was like some runic curse due to which there is neither Arrival nor Departure, nor even a taxi, or even any reality at all. Pilsen was a shock and a counter-shock.

By instinct I found my waiting father, even though he did not emit any light. But it was father.

We rode home on the tram.

And it was an entirely logical road towards light.

And it continues to this day.

The duties of a dustbin

To take up all post-Bolshevik baroque,
balderdash, barnacles, bankruptcies, barristers' wigs.

To catalyze the resurrection
of saints and penguins, who until then

quarrelled below the lid
and darkly tapped the window
at the conjunction of Venus and Mars.

To testify how things were
before the starmakers arrived.

To safeguard the black-and-white dog's head
for overworked walk-ons.

Because, surprisingly, even they still hold
some things sacred.

The secret life of steam locomotives

The secret life of steam locomotives is not only intensive but also relatively easy to understand, because these engines breathe in and out, with sharp eyes watch the free run of the landscape and reflect on it with white puffs of locomotive awareness. Their massive muscles with black sinewy linkages are for many hours tensed to bursting point. Small wonder that afterwards they repair to their accommodations, which are known as engine sheds or engine barns and provide a kind of substitute home for them; basically railway engines are foundlings without a home town or a native hearth.

That's why they carry their hearth inside them, in the region of their hot pelvic bones.

In Pilsen most of the engines lived behind the marshalling yard, above Roudná, and awakening from their sleep they would raise or incline their steamy soul towards the little church of St George, which shivered in a variety of transformations since the Romanesque period down below the embankment by the Mže river. However, the patron saint of steam engines is not St George but St Dragon, and what people regard as St George-like is really dragon-like. In all sculptures the dragon is tendentiously reduced in size to some psittosaurus or fabrosaurus belonging to the ornithoschians, whereas in fact he must have been a sauroschian Tyrannosaurus, against whom even a saint on horseback was in the position of Pa Smurf on a grasshopper. Steam engines are the legitimate successors of Tyrannosauruses and they don't love the birdlike survivors of that other line.

To this day the engines, as far as the track will permit, pursue chickens for persiflage and as a ridiculous diminution of their dinosauric Jurassic and Cretaceous period.

The Pilsen locomotives, having woken up in their engine sheds, roll out to work on a single track, or at least did so when I was with the railways. I can attest that an engine is an inspired and unique creature in the manner of the prophet Jochanaan or Tristan Tzara. Its whereabouts cannot be recorded by some stupid bureaucratic register or by a soulless automaton, but have to be recorded daily by some railway bird-watcher. When I was on the staff the Jurassic locomotives of the 365, 524, and even 354 series would roll out of their shed in the morning and, having prayed to St Dinosaur, move on for service in the marshalling yard or at the passenger or freight station. Along the track from the shed stood a little hut for the observation and recording of the awakened engines; this contained a bare table, a small chair and a stubble-faced bird-watcher with a wooden leg, who had been doing this job continuously for the past ten years, in the course of which he had become unaccustomed to human speech and only occasionally whistled under his beard. The engines, proud as ever, did not slow down past his little hut, pretending to be unaware of him. But he surmised them.

When an awakened engine appeared in the distance, or a group of engines, the prophet would limp out of his hut with an asthmatic wheeze and go halfway to the track. There he would remain calmly, only now and again shaking his head. He only returned when the whole group had passed.

He would then sit down with a grating sound at his little table and with an exceptionally blunt pencil scribble into a lined copybook the numbers 422 0112, 354 1106, 354 1109, 275 0133, 365 1013, 475 0254, 354 0245. Sometimes seven and sometimes ten locomotives at a time.

Having been introduced as an educated type, I relieved him. I discovered that it was impossible for the sake of a single engine to run out and back again, because another engine would then pass unrecorded. I got two engines mixed up at the fourth digit already and when five of them passed I was no longer sure if there had been five or seven, besides one of them could have been an open-top gondola or the head of the marshalling yard.

In the course of the morning I missed about twenty-five engines, while on the other hand I created about fifteen engines which never existed and never will exist. While it did not exactly cause an upheaval in the transport situation, it was a flagrant infringement of the ritual which is part of the life of the locomotives. At midday I was relieved by a superannuated locomotive checker, who was more talkative and mobile, but even more stubble-faced and with a glass eye. As a matter of principle he addressed the traffic inspector as Annie, though in fact he was a male and his name was Morák.

The engine checker undoubtedly recorded the engines also by their breathing and the squeaking of their linked wheels, and he knew them by their Christian names, like Albatross, Hunchback and Parrot.

The secret life of steam locomotives fills me to this day with respect and terror of their noisy unknowable.

A man with an education can do a lot. But if he retains his sanity he'll discover in the later phases of his life that he can't do everything.

Tender souls in tough bodies *

The melancholy stationmaster
of Spičák
was recently found in the tunnel.
His head severed by a train.

When they brought him out a linesman
carefully
placed his cap on his head.

* from the Czech national anthem, second stanza.

402 Muskets

'By a fortunate chance the ancient town armory has been preserved in Pilsen and is today our most precious treasure. Whereas other towns and museums can boast of only one or at best a handful of firearms from the 15th or early 16th centuries, our museum possesses 402 of them. You may well find more beautiful and more valuable collections of weapons elsewhere, but nowhere in the world will you find four hundred genuine battle muskets which were genuinely fired at the Hussite armies or those of George of Poděbrady or even in raids on the neighbouring nobility in the Jagellonian age; because anywhere in the world, except in Pilsen, they would have thrown these weapons onto the scrap heap as long as four hundred years ago.'

These words by Dr Fridolín Macháček were accompanied by 100 drawings by Karel Živný in the work *Pilsen*, published by Theodor Mareš, bookseller, in 1929. The copy in question, in a blue cloth binding by Mr Kobeš, was kept on our family shelves. I never devoted much attention either to this work or to the museum; in fact the first time I stepped into the museum in my life was when I myself had become an exhibit. And not so long ago I discovered that while there may be 402 muskets and suchlike inside, on top of the building there are no longer those three typical turrets which some Pilsen architectural giant evidently lifted off and dropped into the grass in the park next to the petrified tree trunks or araucarites.

I regret this disinterest of mine. Just think how these 402 five-hundred-year-old muskets might have changed my attitude to the town which, for its loyalty, was exempted from taxes and from Bohemian and Bavarian customs duties by King Sigismund, which was granted a second annual fair by King George, but nevertheless opposed him, so that for ten years it not only hosted the Prague Catholic Chapter, which resulted in a remarkable boom for business, but also received from the Pope the right to use red sealing wax, and on top of it all managed to preserve all those guns and create a collection unique in the world. What a clever town!

And its luck held. Some 20,000 head of Pilsen cattle were driven into Bavaria in the sixteenth century and according to the tax returns of 1557 Pilsen was the second most wealthy city in Bohemia.

And its luck held. Under Rudolph II the Pilsen lobby obtained a great many privileges and Rudolph even made Pilsen his imperial residence for nine months during 1599-1600, when the plague was raging in Prague. He even graciously built an enclosed balcony on Sebastian Pechovský's house so he should have a better view. A clever city, even though Rudolph cost it some money.

And Pilsen's luck held even when, during the rebellion of the estates, it was captured by Mansfeld, but somehow it came to terms with him.

And it continued to hold during the epidemics of syphilis, anthrax and smallpox in the seventeenth century, when considerably fewer witches, succubuses and incubuses and considerably more real adulteresses and women murderers of illegitimate children were burnt in Pilsen than anywhere else.

And Pilsen's luck continued to hold.

On the place of execution of Jan Sladký Kozina, the leader of a Chod rebellion, the brewery was built and the tower of the brewery's waterworks dominates the northeastern horizon like a well-deserved plague column.

And it continued to hold during the wars of the eighteenth century, when the occupation forces and others providing fraternal help were bought off with an astonishingly small sum.

And it continued to hold when for the third time the city 'gratefully received' Josef Kajetán Tyl, giving him a decent burial, moreover with the effect that suddenly a large number of loyal Czechs appeared in Pilsen who until then had kept rather hidden.

And it still held when in 1869 Emil Škoda bought the Waldstein engineering plant and the town hall welcomed the deal even though the mayor made no personal profit from it. What a clever city!

And it continued to hold when, with a chance foresight over a distance of forty years we allowed ourselves to be liberated by Generals Patton and Roberts and Harmon, while a little further to the east Czech civilians and lyrically glorious little Soviet soldiers had to die so that some bearded idols with ideas of world rule should have their way. Today we are again profiting from this fact, with significant support from the Bolshevik paranoia which, in the fifties, in the triangle formed by Jungmann Street and the Avenue of Czech Legionaries, demolished even that small stone laid by the American Institute, reminding us that America exists.

The weapons from that American episode are not preserved in the museum because the Americans merely lent them to us. Even though, probably due to my Pilsen blood, I had traded a crock of lard for an American 7.65 calibre pistol, but my father took it from me and buried it in the garden.

If I make a big effort I get the feeling that my Czech (and hence basically Protestant) soul is reconciled with this clever city just because of that American episode. History experienced is rather different from history described, and that which in books may appear as treachery, astuteness, defeat, victory, loyalty, cleverness, pragmatism, zeal, left-wing-ness, ineptitude or aptitude, appears so largely due to the position or point of view of the book in question, and not of life as such, life on this earth, life at that time.

And so I accept those 402 historical muskets more gladly than the red sealing wax. Besides, these muskets were used less often than the sealing wax and thus, in a sense, stood outside history, as an a-priori monument.

As for the ancient city armory, our most precious treasure, I am keeping it in my personal inner consciousness as evidence that we didn't go totally idiotic under any regime, but remembered the potential significance of old ironmongery.

Executions

Jan Sladký, known as Kozina,
was hanged in November 1695
on the spot where today
stands the brewery's water-tower.
A scrap of his body remained on the rope
for a whole year
for the eyes of the city
as a lesson.

A few robber barons
dutifully beheaded in the square.
A few witches were burnt.
A few adulteresses and newborn babes
were strangled.

And to this day.

You only have to
look into people's eyes, and inside are
squares,
breweries,
cages,
gags,
dry wood.
A tiny, permanent hangman.

A scrap of a body behind the eyes
as a lesson
to others.

'Haven't you heard, you dumb cattle?'

But then, what kind of city would it be, what kind of cradle, what kind of house, what kind of mother and father and the holy ghost of home amen, if they didn't appear in every dream, in every slumber, in every phase of REM, anywhere in the world, in Vancouver as much as at the Kilauea volcano in Hawaii, and in Ohio, just as in Berlin, or in Prague, or in Wilpena Pound, South Australia, in Rotterdam or in Paris, oh yes, and in Russell Square in London or in Washington Square, New York, in Warsaw, in Peking, on Salonika in Greece, or in Barcelona, and in Cluj, and of course in Copenhagen, where the Andersen dogs run about with eyes like millstones, or in Perpignan, where the Letters from my Mill fly through the air, oh yes, Mother's voice is heard everywhere and everywhere we were going to the mountain lake with our parents, what a worry this would be if it weren't a worry about someone ten years dead, what a picture of a possible world this would be if it weren't a futile picture...

I miss such futile pictures in Pilsen; almost as if the local intellectuals were too light-weight and the local property owners too heavy. There are but few traces of Pilsen in Czech literature. *The Chronicle of Troy*, printed here in 1468, is probably our principal monument, and that originated elsewhere.

There is a certain tradition in this. In 1992, in the Gerhart Hauptmann House in Düsseldorf, I met Gertrud Fussenegger, a diabolical woman of eighty, evidently immortal, who was born in Pilsen and has celebrated Pilsen in a family novel, *The House of Dark Jugs*, 1951, and now, with a voice of kettle-drums and tubas, calls on her neighbours not to behave like fat black rats... *The House of Dark Jugs* is a novel from the pre-prewar history of my city, unknown in my city even though it is unique and substantial. The novel says... Anyway, here is a city, painstakingly and systematically built, fairly ancient but, let's admit it, unremarkable like a thousand others... Its navel is the square market place, called the Square... with a church in the middle with a very high steeple. A cathedral from the Gothic period, but it too was built without any particular effort or genius, inside tall and long and bare, with a rosy-cheeked madonna on the high altar.

The history of this city reads like a monotonous but carefully documented event. What adventures occurred there it mostly discharged with some credit, if only because it did not permit itself any extravagance but clung to familiar soundness. That's why it long ago acquired the epithet *The Loyal*, or even *The Ever-Loyal*. It probably had rectitude and propriety from the beginnings, because it cost a modest piece of farmland, good for potatoes and brewing barley...

The god Gambrinus is a comfortable god, moderating even those who invoke him; his vapours are unpropitious for revolutions, upheavals, and even moral courage...

In this city – according to the gospel of Gertrud Fussenegger and all other gospel-true accounts, all of them equally probable and equally neutral and traditional – coming 'from the western wooded regions', settled the Bourdanin or Pourdanin ancestors, printers of massive stature, thanks to which, 190 years ago, they married into the privilege of brewing beer, and thus Joseph Bourdanin became the co-founder of the Municipal Brewery, his son Balthasar Bourdanin married the daughter of burgomaster Silbernagel and, out of sheer enthusiasm, printed and published a history of Bohemia, a textbook of mathematics, an explorer's travel account and even a slim volume of poetry, of which he sold exactly seventeen copies, though closest to his heart, but then every publisher says just that, but unlike most publishers Balthasar Bourdanin won the lottery, so that the municipal cattleherd proclaimed in the Square (quoted literally from Fussenegger), *Haven't you heard, you dumb cattle, that Balthasar's won?* – with the result that Balthasar bought several houses and moved into the Cameralium (something like a municipal office) and in the revolutionary year of 1848 even became mayor of the city, and when the revolution was crushed he at least introduced gas lighting, a public water supply and an orphanage.

And thus the brewing-charter destiny of the Bourdanins and Pilsen continued to unroll and be preserved in brewing-charter cellars and dark jugs, celebrated by Gertrud Fussenegger in Austria and Germany, while the less brewing-charterish destiny of my town hasn't so far been written, or even celebrated, or even belittled, and that is why I here take the liberty of publicly proclaiming – being neither a brewer nor a burgher nor even a conservative Ever-Loyal, but a genetic Protestant – that the picture of Pilsen as the City of Malt is just as nonsensical as that of the City of Rectitude.

I take the liberty of publicly proclaiming: Haven't you heard, you dumb cattle, that we've neither won nor lost, but are trying to get an orphanage? And not behave exclusively like fat black rats?

Pilsen's principal metaphor – the doorway to the brewery. I've never been there in my life, but I like the thought that behind such a hideous doorway they switched to bottom fermentation as early as the 19th century. Bottom fermentation somehow suggests poetry. [FD]

Central cemetery

Ludicrously contorted figures
fly through the chimney, shedding soot
and settling in the tombs
without any certainty of
who is who.

Mortuus semper incertus.

Invigorated with humus
after midnight they raise the lids
of sarcophagi and with their right hand grope
for the headstone in case there's a name there.

But at that moment an emaciated monkey
is sitting on the tomb and the hand
gullibly roams over its vertebrae.

Adieu, adieu, remember me,
moans Hamlet, because there's nothing
left, not even a footprint.
Just a drop of earthly oil,
a cranial suture
and a dream like a ladder
in the sock of history.

Senza traccia.

Abandon hope, you asses.
And this is only that evangelical phase
when we're abandoning our clan
and become a city.

The metaphysics of beer

One New Year's Eve, at Špičák in the Šumava mountains, there was much shouting and howling at the tavern by the school. A totally drunk male mountain-dweller was being chased around the house by a totally infuriated female mountain-dweller who, screaming, called upon Christ Almighty and invoked the hungry mouths of her children and her cow back home. The two of them in turn fell down into the yellowish and blotchy snow. The Bavarian dialect was reflected back from a lowering sky and fell upon our heads like ash. Bavarian beer combined with Bavarian abuse and universal despair.

I didn't develop any liking either for the beer or for the pub. And whenever Father sent me out with a glass jug to get his beer in Pilsen, the bleary eyes and replete cursing voices of the well-oiled regulars, combining with the plague-like stench of a Czech pub, seemed to me somewhat Bavarian. And it seemed to me that until the beer was drawn and decapitated with a knife I was inside the stomach of a Carthaginian battle elephant.

I appreciate Pilsen beer just as I do the tower of St Bartholomew's church, from which, however, I don't have to jump just because of my appreciation. I also regard it as exceptionally appropriate that Pilsen beer was established in the year of our Lord 1842 by Joseph Groll, a Bavarian, the son of a brewer from Wilshofen, the worst bastard and rudest of all Bavarian brewers, who were only too happy to export him. Besides, he didn't remain in Pilsen long, all that remained was the beer, which replaced the swipes until then manufactured by the chartered brewers of Pilsen and, by an exemplary gesture, emptied 36 barrels in the Square in 1838 at the behest of the townhall and to the vituperations of those affected.

I believe that the magic of Pilsen beer is in the character of the water, the cellars and Groll's technology. But those little bubbles are probably neighbourly Czech-Bavarian insults.

Pompeii

In Pompeii,
down the bumpy pavement
of Venus Street,
under a full antique sun
Red Riding Hood drags
her basket of gifts.

Such a beautiful moment.

Grandmother has
genital herpes, but
doesn't know what it is.

Mixed into the cake
is cholera.
But the centurions
don't believe in infection.

Such beautiful times.
In the distance
Vesuvius rumbles and
marsh gas is burning,
but geology
ended with Empedocles
in the crater of Etna.

Such a perfect epoch.

The glow-worm 'gins to pale
his uneffectual fire.
Soon
they will all be baked
into petrified mud like
currants of immortality,

and during excavations will be heard
chorales of wolves, Hamlets and concubines
about the good old days.

The ancient door to which the brewing privilege was tied and on which
the concierge had written KEEP CLOSED. But most of the time it was
half open, to let some fresh air in... [VR]

Fragrances

Mr Mareš's bookshop was on Jungmann Street, later there was a furniture shop, which was remarkable for the fact that they had no furniture, whereas Mr Mareš's bookshop was remarkable for the fact that they did have two kinds books there. Out in front were the books officially permitted, behind the shop in the storeroom on long and crowded shelves were the less permitted and non-permitted books.

And these books smelled.

I don't know if they smelled through being forbidden or because of the time of their production, or through being concentrated in an unventilated store, but they had a fragrance like French bread, for they were the books of surrealists and Freudians, they smelled like black pepper, for they were the books of Kipling and Faulkner, they smelled like smoked salmon, for they were the books of Melville and St Exupéry, they smelled like steel and steam, for they were the works of Sandburg and Frost or Eliot (T.S.), they smelled like violets and sprouting grain, for they were the writings of Seifert and Nezval.

The whole store then had a dedicated book smell which was on a par with the fragrance of grass, of soil and of silver winds. It was a fragrance that was both indefinable and unforgettable, even though our relevant sensory cells are being replaced every moment.

Young Mr Mareš, or perhaps subMareš, would let me hang about there for hours. He would wrap up the volumes I selected behind a curtain, so that I would leave the shop with an anonymous package at which I would sniff pleasurably, afraid that it might evaporate. It didn't evaporate.

Those writings haven't evaporated to this day.

Just as the forests won't evaporate. Or bakers' shops. Or meadows. Or drapery and ammonium chloride.

Or the kitchen back home in the morning when Mother in course of resurrection was laying the fire in the stove, in the words of Mr Holan, whose books then smelled of the black plumage of protobirds, rooks and enchanted princesses.

Reading

Before I fell asleep Mother would read me
Jean Christophe, page by page,
like Beethoven falling silent and
a green harp being found. In the fifth part
we finished on page 244.

I went off to fall asleep in another sea,
in another bathyscape.

But Mother no doubt is reading on, somewhere
in the blue room with the picture of breaking waves
in a golden frame, with a cut-glass vase
on the table, with the eye of a young Leviathan at the window,
the hoarse clock on the graveyardlike wardrobe,
the mummies of dictionaries and the skeletons of saltshakers.

She reads in rolling spacetime,
where Notre Dame and Rue Royal Navarin
blend with the rusty little churches in Bohemia
and with the tramcars on Klatovská Street,
where Romain Rolland is an assistant in
Mr Kavan's grocer's shop and Napoleon
assembles his forces to conquer the brewing privilege,

for such is the custom of immortality
of a poet's work, such is the invariant relation
in Mandelbrot's equations,
such is the recreational regime in Hades.

I don't understand what she reads. But when
I awaken I always remember the last
two or three words. And the squeal of the last tramcar
on Klatovská.

Prévert's lazy schoolboy will 'draw the face of happiness/ with chalks of every colour/ on the blackboard of unhappiness'. The street along which I used to go home from school: in Mr Šimandl's stationery shop they used to sell coloured chalks. [MH]

Deukalion's people

Deukalion, along with his wife Pyrrha, saved himself from the dis-
astrous world-wide flood and repopulated the world with the bones
of his mother, i.e. with stones which, together with madam, he
cast behind him. The stones which Pyrrha threw turned into
women, the stones which Deukalion threw turned into men. In
1943 this scene was painted by Mr Šíma, though he disregarded
the fact that Deukalion threw with both hands, alternatively; when
he flung with his left he produced ordinary men, when he flung
with his right he created footballers.

Quite a few of those stones rolled towards Pilsen.

Those were lesser stones, well-smoothed, in a sense technically
gifted and nervously unstable.

Myself I am clearly descended from the left-hand throws, which
is why I have undying sympathy for the right-hand ones. And
although at a long-distant encounter between Victoria Pilsen and
Slavia Prague my father had instructed me to root for the red-and-
white side, because the red-and-blue of the Pilsen team caused
him political embarrassment, I have ever since firmly supported
Victoria.

I realised that while with Jove's permission some very fine men
arose after the Flood, such as Pericles, the Elder Pliny, Marcus
Aurelius, Dante, Leonardo, Newton and Kundera, these were
really only alternatives to such men as Bína, Hess, Čulík, Bešták,
Vlček, Perk, the Sloup brothers and above all the goal-keepers; of
one of these, Jabornický, at one of the few glorious moments of
my life, I won a photograph in the football chocolate competition
organised by Lido, as gratefully remembered by our eminent jour-
nalist Jiří Ruml, who also comes from my part of the world. At
that moment I positively felt the warmth of Deukalion's palm; I
was illumined by the fact that he was the son of Prometheus and
after the Flood landed on the slopes of Mount Parnassus.

There must have been quite a lot of mud there.

Besides, who can be sure that Deukalion didn't run out of stones
and began to help himself to some softer material. On the slopes
of Parnassus I sometimes have just that feeling.

And I am also sure that on the slopes of Parnassus few have any
idea of what it means to score a goal.

It also seems to me that only Deukalion's people from the orig-
inal harder material have any idea of what it means to win.

On the origin of football

A small pebble embedded in concrete:
a statue to the genius of earthworms,
not budging at all.

A small milestone of history,
such a tiny little
triumphal arch
where nothing has ever happened:
not budging at all.

A small rheumatic post
from which someone has stolen the notice
forbidding the stealing of notices:
not budging at all.

An electrified wire
barbedly garrisoning
the dreams of shin ulcers:
not budging at all.

And so, when one day someone encounters
something that's rolling
he kicks it.

And his heavens reverberate,
the temple curtain is rent,
the unrinsed mouths of thousands open wide
in a stifling explosion of silence

like trilobites
yelling *Goal!*

Aida

Whenever in the Winter Stadium Pilsen scores a goal in ice hockey they play a few bars of the triumphal march from *Aida*. Over the past thirty years I have seen *Aida* about four times – in New York, in Berlin, in London, and in Prague near the railway station at that theatre that is forever called something different.

But I never heard the march sound more gloriously than in that Winter Stadium which, unlike most opera houses, is reached after a lot of slipping on ice, or through a swamp, or at best over a pavement reminiscent of graves opening on Judgement Day.

Aida sounds best of all during hockey matches in Pilsen.

May this heresy be charged against my eternal life.

Besides, you can't win in eternity anyway, not even in extra time.

Mother is learning Spanish

She started when she was
eighty-two. On page 26
she invariably dozed off.
Algo se trama.

The pencil for underlining the verbs
strayed embarrassedly over the page,
drawing hairline contours of death.
No hay necesidad de respuestas.

It traced the routes
of Hernán Cortés' errands.
It drew El Greco's eye.
It drew Picasso's fish
larger than its aquarium.

A self-willed pencil
like Fuente Ovejuna.
Like a bull in the Plaza de Toros Monumental arena,
when it is down on its knees
and the horse team sets out.

No hay necesidad de respuestas.
There's no need for reply.
Again.

She sleeps now.

While Gaudí
in her honour
failed to complete the
cathedral Sagrada Familia.

Winds

Old Mathers in Flann O'Brien's *Third Policeman* says: 'No doubt you are aware that the winds have colours.'

I wasn't.

'A record of this belief will be found in the literature of all ancient peoples.'

(Perhaps he was referring to de Selby's famous theory, according to which night is not caused by the movements of planets at all, but by an accumulation of 'black air' generated by certain volcanic activities.)

'There are four winds and eight sub-winds, each with its own colour. The wind from the east is a deep purple, from the south a fine shining silver. The north wind is a hard black and the west wind is amber. People in the old days had the power of perceiving these colours and could spend a day sitting quietly on a hillside watching the beauty of the winds, their fall and rise and changing hue, the magic of neighbouring winds when they are interweaved like ribbons at a wedding. It was a better occupation than gazing at newspapers. The sub-winds had colours of indescribable delicacy, a reddish-yellow half-way between silver and purple, a greyish-green which was related equally to black and brown. What could be more exquisite than a countryside swept lightly by cool rain reddened by the south-west breeze!'

You were asking me what my colour was. How do people get their colours?

'A person's colour,' he answered slowly, 'is the colour of the wind prevailing at his birth.'

What is your own colour?

'Light yellow.'

And what is the point of knowing your colour or having a colour at all?

'For one thing you can tell the length of your life from it. Yellow means a long life and the lighter the better.'

This is very edifying, every sentence a sermon in itself. Please explain.

'It is a question of making little gowns,' he said informatively.

Little gowns?

'Yes. When I was born there was a certain policeman present who had the gift of wind-watching. The gift is getting very rare these days. Just after I was born he went outside and examined the colour of the wind that was blowing across the hill. He had a secret bag with him full of certain materials and bottles and he had tailor's instruments also. He was outside for about ten minutes. When he came in again he had a little gown in his hand and he made my mother put it on me.'

Where did he get this gown? I asked in surprise.

'He made it himself secretly in the backyard, very likely in the cowhouse. It was very thin and slight like the very finest spider's muslin. You would not see it at all if you held it against the sky but at certain angles of the light you might at times accidentally notice the edge of it. It was the purest and most perfect manifestation of the outside skin of pale yellow. This yellow was the colour of my birth-wind.'

I see, I said. A very beautiful conception.

'Every time my birthday came,' old Mathers said, 'I was presented with another little gown of the same identical quality except that it was put on over the other one and not in place of it. You may appreciate the extreme delicacy and fineness of the material when I tell you that even at five years old with five of these gowns together on me, I still appeared to be naked. It was, however, an unusual yellowish sort of nakedness. Of course there was no objection to wearing other clothes over the gown. I usually wore an overcoat. But every year I got a new gown.'

Where did you get them? I asked.

'From the police. They were brought to my home until I was big enough to call at the barracks for them.'

And how does all this enable you to predict your span of life?

'I will tell you. No matter what your colour is, it will be represented faithfully in your birth-gown. With each year and each gown, the colour will get deeper and more pronounced. In my own case I had attained a bright full-blown yellow at fifteen although the colour was so light at birth as to be imperceptible. I am now nearing seventy and the colour is a light brown. As my gowns come to me through the years ahead, the colour will deepen to dark brown, then to a dull mahogany and from that ultimately to that very dark sort of brownness one associated usually with stout.'

'In a word, the colour gradually deepens gown by gown and year by year until it appears to be black. Finally a day will come when the addition of one further gown will actually achieve real and full blackness. On that day I will die.'

That means, I said at last, that if you get a number of these gowns and put them all on together, reckoning each as a year of life, you can ascertain the year of your death?

'Theoretically yes,' he replied, 'but there are two difficulties. First of all the police refuse to let you have the gowns together on the ground that the general ascertainment of death-days would be contrary to the public interest. They talk of breaches of the peace and so forth. Secondly, there is a difficulty about stretching.'

Stretching?

'Yes. Since you will be wearing as a grown man the tiny gown that fitted you when you were born, it is clear that the gown has stretched until it is perhaps one hundred times as big as it was originally. Naturally this will affect the colour, making it many times rarer than it was. Similarly there will be a proportional stretch and a corresponding diminution in colour in all the gowns up to manhood – perhaps twenty or so in all.'

I take it then that from the colour of your shirt you can tell roughly whether you will be long-lived or short-lived?

'Yes. But if you use your intelligence you can make a very accurate forecast. Naturally some colours are better than others. Some of them, like purple or maroon, are very bad and always mean an early grave. Pink, however, is excellent, and there is a lot to be said for certain shades of green and blue. The prevalence of such colours at birth, however, usually connote a wind that brings bad weather – thunder and lightning, perhaps – and there might be difficulties such, for instance, as getting a woman to come in time. As you know, most good things in life are associated with certain disadvantages.'

Who are these policemen? I asked.

'There is Sergeant Pluck and another man called MacCruiskeen, and then there is a third man called Fox that disappeared twenty-five years ago and was never heard of after. The first two are down in the barracks, and so far as I know they have been there for hundreds of years. They must be operating on a very rare colour, something that ordinary eyes could not see at all. There is no white wind that I know of. They all have the gift of seeing the winds.'

Proceeding systematically from the scientific contributions of Flann O'Brien and Professor de Selby I should like to point out that the four colours of the Pilsen coat of arms essentially refer to the four principal winds: top left the southerly, white; top right the westerly, yellow; bottom left the northerly mixed up with a few subwinds giving a sort of green, the camel on a black ground would be a reminder that it is essentially of black market origin, since the Taborites requisitioned it in Poland and the people of Pilsen, according to tradition, stole it from the Taborites; bottom right then the east wind, red, not too vigorous, so as to match the age of a leaping greyhound. The keys top left could of course have come from Pope Paul II, but only for the sake of concealment. In actual fact they are the keys of the police barracks where the gowns are kept and where two intrepid policemen on the one hand, top right, are trimming half a spread-eagle, which is an allegory for the policeman's favourite means of transport, the bicycle, while on the other hand one of them is standing right in the middle of the gate in order to control the black air and all passers-by, and chiefly, and quite obviously, he is standing there on top of the gate grasping two banners, his instruments for checking the prevailing wind. That policeman on top of the gate is the Third Policeman, he is wearing a gown, or a sweatshirt of the colour of good dark beer and watches the prospects of your longevity when you get within a distance of less than eight feet and two inches, moreover after you've ingested Martin Kopecký's curative Lochotín water.

In case this clear exposition does not satisfy some scientific sceptic, let me draw attention to the participation of the Irish, from whose clan came also Mr O'Brien, in Wallenstein's entourage, who between November 1633 and 21 February 1634, when they were in Pilsen, received two pounds of meat and two litres of beer daily, who numbered 899 men and 1072 horses and who at the famous Scribonius house in the Square observed the prevailing winds.

As for the role of policemen, surely none of us has had any doubts since the discovery of the heliocentricity of our planetary system.

The Pilsen coat-of-arms. [MH]

Half a hedgehog

The rear half had been run over,
leaving the head and thorax
and the front legs of the hedgehog shape.

A scream from a cramped-open
jaw. The scream of the mute is
more horrible than the silence after a flood,
when even black swans float
belly upwards.

And even if some hedgehog doctor were
to be found in a hollow trunk or under the leaves
in a beechwood there'd be no hope
for that mere half on Road E12.

In the name of logic,
in the name of the theory of pain,
in the name of the hedgehog god the father, the son
and the holy ghost amen,
in the name of games and unripe raspberries,
in the name of tumbling streams of love
ever different and ever bloody,
in the name of the roots which overgrow
the heads of aborted foetuses,
in the name of satanic beauty,
in the name of skin bearing human likeness,
in the name of all halves
and double helices, of purines
and pyrimidines

we tried to run over
the hedgehog's head with the front wheel.

And it was like guiding a lunar module
from a planetary distance,
from a control centre seized
by cataleptic sleep.

And the mission failed. I got out
and found a heavy piece of brick.
Half the hedgehog continued screaming. And now
the scream turned into speech,

prepared by
the vaults of our tombs:
Then death will come and it will have your eyes.

The triumph of death

For houses become tombs and cities become a chorale of demented skeletons.

A house in which a man with asthma lies has dirty windows.

A house in which cardiac arrest occurs sheds its plaster in syncope.

A house which conceals kidney failure has lost some tiles.

A house where pneumonia reigns has a leaky roof.

A house disintegrates along with its occupants. A house is a projection of terror of the end. A house is a clogging of veins and the clogging of veins is the loss of the key to the glass door.

In a house where a man dies in his bed the ceilings crack in the semblance of runes and the tufts of hair on the floorboards turn into terrible chickens of destruction.

And a woman roams from room to room, asking what has become of Descartes' words about method and of Voltaire's words about laughter.

A dead man's house quivers and withers like a den in a north wind.

In the cellar someone breaks a little window and robs the cabinet of our childhood, for there is nothing left now in the house except time past. Gold and silver have been carried away by others.

Then the thin-walled angel steps into the door and lets nothing pass either in or out. Death is a black hole that sucks in all living matter and living logic.

The house will never be the same as before the death, even if new fates move in and the blue room is turned into a while hall. Somewhere the black hole of the anti-house will always be lurking and at night a rustling of bones and of shrouds will be heard.

And as the generations change, so the houses fill with ever new anti-houses, with chickens of destruction, with holes after the carrying-off of Faustuses and with holes after the murder of demons.

Thus cities brimming with life are in fact brimming over with death. For death in the likeness of walls, stairs, door-frames and corners is much more enduring and impressive.

If quietly and alone you take a long look at a city in the evening you'll see Brueghel's picture of The Triumph of Death.

All the more you'll appreciate that you still have muscles on your bones. They won't stay. And your soul will turn into tufts of hair on long unpolished floors, as demanded by the gospel of the house and the city.

Requiem

He got up so lightly
that he didn't appear in the mirror,
he shuffled across the shabby floorboards,
which were beginning to crack,
he closed the door to the landing,
where a picture of the Black Lake
was beginning to fade,
he descended the stairs
with their worn carpet,
in the hall, where a light-bulb had gone,
he turned off the switch, for safety,
he double-locked the front door,
took a last look at the garden,
shut the half-rotten gate
and limping vanished into the street,

which led to a street,
which led to streets,
which led to all streets,
which led to the infinitely crooked strets

of his native town.

Wenceslas II only just made it

I have become a Meritorious Native of Pilsen. I was given a silver medal and at the final evening of the celebrations of the 700th anniversary of the foundation of our city (1295-1995) I had to make the prize draw for a Chrysler car, I have forgotten the name of the model, because the thought that I should pick one lucky person among 77,000 less lucky ones depressed me.

I discovered that I was from Pilsen to such an extent that next time round I must be born there again.

I was full of pride, together with the seven-hundred-year-old city. It should be pointed out that feeling pride in the post-Communist era is rather rare; most of the time people are whinging that they are not yet doing all that well, even though relatively they are doing very well, and they whinge chiefly because under the Communists whinging wasn't permitted.

While preparing for its celebrations the town progressed in two years by about fifteen, the evil spirits vanished, as did the crumbling plaster and the unplastered citizens, the new façades of old buildings are sparkling, there is the greatest concentration of entrepreneurs per square kilometre of the whole country, one is building, one is getting younger, so that, as Jiří Suchý put it, the town really doesn't look its seven hundred years, more like five hundred.

As the celebrations of the city's foundation by Henry the Founder, a subject of Wenceslas II of the House of the Přemyslides, progressed I again realised how lucky the city has been. Just imagine if Wenceslas II had been a little quicker about founding New Pilsen, say by a mere seven or eight years. The Gothic city with its streets arranged at right angles would probably be much the same, but the celebrations would have had to follow the Russian liturgy, under which even right angles were not recognised.

In that case our celebrations in 1987 would have included: installation of a red star on the tower of St Bartholomew's church; construction of a Potemkin village immediately beyond Božkov; decorations for several Red Army men who had served incognito in the US Army. And finally the historical discovery that the foundation had really been the idea of the Rurik dynasty in Russia, passed on to Wenceslas II by the merchant Yakov before he was put in the stocks for the sale of fake furs. And plaster would still be crumbling and the town would be sliding, like a squinting eye, towards the right, towards the Urals.

When you get down to brass tacks in history you realise how terribly important good timing is. And Wenceslas II only just made it.

Good King Wenceslases

Wenceslas IV, King of Bohemia,
felled at Kunratice by his second heart attack,
after being hidden for a month ended up
in the royal tomb in Zbraslav.

After a year the tomb was looted
by Hussite mobs from Prague, the insignia stolen,
bones scattered about the church, so that
Wenceslas III was never found again and
Wenceslas IV, who was still in one piece,
was placed on the altar, wreathed with hay and straw
and to great general enjoyment filled up with good beer
through his part-decayed oral orifice.

When the popular festivity was over
his corpse was dragged out by a certain fisherman
and buried in a vineyard. After three years he then
handed over some bones from the vineyard
for solemn interment.

As a result we are short
in the Cathedral of one or two
King-Wenceslases
and, as always, we have a surplus
of one heart attack, one festivity

and a lot of last-rite beer.

What to ink out

Each time the shutters came down some ministry of memories was instructed to issue new rules, under which libraries had to be purged of the books of Jewish Bolsheviks, or of Masaryk-Beneš-ites, or of bourgeois nationalists and revisionists, or of Papists and formal geneticists. Einstein got it in the neck each time. Our science master Pokorny had a flowing black cloak and a paradichlorobenzene-saturated cabinet, where he collected bits of rock on a wooden tray and stuffed goshawks, or tapeworms preserved in brine for use as teaching aids. I remember that tapeworms were permitted under all regimes, and indeed they are still.

At a particular period Professor Pokorný had to ink out even gypsies and Darwin in our natural history textbook, which he did with officially supplied Indian ink and with firm strokes. This inking out resulted in exceedingly strange and inspirational sentence shapes, of the kind 'The discovery of and search for new elements was largely due to the outstanding chemist......(1834-1907)', or 'From......'s teachings and on the strength of...skeletal finds from man's early history it emerged that... and that present-day man evolved...from more primitive ancestors', or 'The......originated in India and immigrated to Europe in the 10th century. They call themselves......' Considering that even the original non-inked-out sentences were imbued with an elegance of their own, the inking-out produced riddles of unique cognitional value.

I came to the conclusion that in our cities, too, we should always in turn ink out something or other, here a Brown House, there a Red House, which as a rule was the same house, quite certainly the Annunciation or the Ascension, definitely the Franciscan monastery and sometimes the Working Men's House. This would give rise to a very interesting topography which would stick in the memory even of quite casual and hurried foreign visitors. Above Pilsen one might also ink out Radyné as a people-unfriendly and dungeon-equipped creation of an otherwise admissible feudal system with imperial aspirations, as well as the brewing-charter gates of 29 Malá Street, complete with the inhabitants of the house, who, duly inked, might profitably pretend to be the surviving descendants of the Moors from the days of Rudolph II.

And perhaps each one of us might personally ink out something or other. I, for instance, Bezovka Street, where an overbearing older student, subsequently the head of a Prague District Housing

Authority – these things just grow with a person – began to take away my scooter, which I used to ride at two thirty to meet my dad coming from his office, or Nerudova Street, where in 1945 some revolutionary or other confiscated my car, so generously given to me by the Americans and which, unfortunately, I didn't know how to drive, or the Pilsen-1 Sokol gym, where as a result of never-ending gymnastic exercises I once made a puddle, or the football pitch in the same place, where Průša, the PT master, once recalled me from the left wing because of my incompetence, and where my classmate Beránek, whom we had to tie to the goal-post because he was afraid of the ball, once broke my nose with a kick off, or the street from the hospital to Doudlevce, where my dad, when he was a little over eighty came off his bike at full tilt, so that he didn't ride on to Šťáhlavy but rode back home to inspect his bike and make sure nothing had happened to it, after all it had cost 860 Kčs, or the crossroads at Rolnická, where a motorcyclist once ran over a dog and once over my father when he was a little over ninety, my father that is, but he walked home because he'd got his suit dirty, and then he went daily to complain to the cop-shop at the Redemptorists' Church, where a tram nearly ran him over again but didn't, and one classroom in the building at Chod Square, where we were often kept in after school, which I found exceedingly irritating, or the morgue at the Central Cemetery, where I found my father when he'd got lost after his death, or the house on Mánesova Street, where my collection of stones was left, as well as a few dirty pots and a few cupboards when someone had walked off with everything else and Mother was in Prague, which she confused with Paris, Železná Ruda and Dubrovník, and the dais at my grammar school where I got a Failed for the third power of something or other, yes, and some cowardice or other, yes, and some anxiety not to sacrifice everything, or not to sacrifice small victories for major defeats, yes, and the dirt at the goods station, yes, and the cowpats on the airfield, yes, and my inability to climb up a pole or do a swing-up on the horizontal bar, yes, and my inability to exchange a better seashell for a worse one when someone implored me so much, oh yes, one could go on inking out until all that was left of a person was that eager would-be hero Cadet Biegler in *The Good Soldier Švejk* or a brother Karamazov in love with Ulalume, when all that was left of a person was the Catcher in the rye and a Daring young man on the flying trapeze, one could go on inking out, but it would only lead to a Sound of Thunder, as Ray Bradbury wrote, or after a journey by Time Machine to 40 years or 60 million years into the past there would remain, on the shoe of a terrified Eckels the flattened body of a Tertiary golden butterfly and this would change the history and hence the state of the world...

'The little butterfly fell to the floor, an exquisite thing, a small thing that could upset balances and knock down a line of small dominoes, then big dominoes, and then gigantic dominoes, all down the years across Time...'

Eckels, who didn't hold out and carried the butterfly off, must be shot like a rat.

To carry off that little butterfly is the same as inking out the Sokol gym or the morgue. Wherefore it is of no consequence to our tiny lives. Wherefore we leave the whole business to the ministries, may Tyrannosaurus Rex be with them! Maybe.

Masterpiece

The only masterpiece
I ever produced
was a picture of the moth Thysania agrippina,
pastels on grey paper.

The reason was that I was never
much good at painting. The essence of art is
that we're not much good at it.

The moth Thysania agrippina
lifted off from the grey cartridge paper
with needle-like antennae extended,

with a plush abdomen like the buttocks
of Hieronymus Bosch's hybrid goblins
with spindly legs on its flattened chests,
like the spectres in Brueghel's
Dulle Griet, it turned into *Dulle Griet*
with a bundle of pots in her bony hand,
it changed into Bodhidharma
with long sleeves,

it was Yin or Shade
and Yang or Light, Chwei or Darkness
and Ming or Brightness, it had
the black colour of water, the ochre of earth,
the blue colour of wood,

I was proud of it like some Antwerp city father
or like the Tenth Patriarch of the Yellow River,

I sprayed it with shellac, which is
the painters' oath on Goethe's *Theory of Colours*,

and then my drawing master carried it off
to his cabinet,
and then I forgot all about it
just as grandmother forgot her false teeth
in the water glass.

ALSO BY MIROSLAV HOLUB

Poems Before & After

COLLECTED ENGLISH TRANSLATIONS

Translated by IAN & JARMILA MILNER,
EWALD OSERS *and* GEORGE THEINER

'Miroslav Holub is one of the half dozen most important poets writing anywhere' – TED HUGHES. 'One of the sanest voices of our time' – A. ALVAREZ.

Miroslav Holub is the Czech Republic's most important poet, and one of her leading scientists. *Poems Before & After* covers thirty years of his poetry.

Before are his poems from the fifties and sixties, poems written *before* the Soviet invasion of Czechoslovakia: first published in English in his Penguin *Selected Poems* and in Bloodaxe's *The Fly*, with some additional poems. **After** are translations of his later poetry, poems written *after* 1968, mostly from his second Bloodaxe selection, *On the Contrary*.

'He is a magnificent, astringent genius and this volume sings with an oblique and cutting candour, a tubular coolness we must praise again and again' – TOM PAULIN.

'A laying bare of things, not so much the skull beneath the skin, more the brain beneath the skull; the shape of relationships, politics, history; the rhythms of affections and disaffection; the ebb and flow of faith, hope, violence, art' – SEAMUS HEANEY.

Paperback: ISBN 1 85224 122 5   £9.95

The Jingle Bell Principle

Translated by JAMES NAUGHTON

Miroslav Holub is known to Czech readers not only as a poet but also as a witty magazine columnist, whose droll musings were especially valued in darker times. When he was a "non-person", these "column articles" weren't published under Holub's own name, but everyone knew who'd written them because the style was immediately recognisable as his: a cross between Flann O'Brien and Jonathan Swift, with a dash of *Tristram Shandy*...the *Beachcomber* of Wenceslas Square.

Subtitled *Notes and objections, maximum length 43 lines*, these "essaylets" are as brilliant and blackly funny as his poetry and as succinct and precisely observed as his scientific writing. In their pausings and musings over daily, supposedly ordinary happenings, they focus on the quirks of human conduct, yet the mirror they prop up to everyday life neither merely distorts nor simply reflects, but pinpoints little facets of human activity which reveal the mortality, thoughts and behaviour of our present age and civilisation.

This selection from Holub's contributions to the magazine *VTM* (maximum length, 43 lines) is illustrated by the leading Czech cartoonist Vladimír Renčín, with photographs by Vojtěch Písařík.

Paperback: ISBN 1 85224 123 3   £7.95

Miroslav Holub was born in Pilsen, Czechoslovakia, in 1923. His father was a lawyer for the railways, his mother a language teacher. In 1942 he was conscripted to work on the railways. After the war he studied medicine at Charles University in Prague. He started his poetic career by taking up a position of total silence after the Communist takeover in 1948. His first poems, influenced by his work as a clinical pathologist, appeared in 1954–56 His first book was published in 1958, the year he received his PhD in immunology from the same Institute of the Academy to which he returned in 1995.

His Czech publications include 16 books of poetry and nine books of essays or sketches. He has also published 162 learned papers on immunology. His scientific publications include the monograph *Immunology of Nude Mice* (CRC Press, Boca Raton, Florida, 1989); his essays on science and culture are collected in *The Dimension of the Present Moment* (Faber & Faber, 1990) and *This Long Disease* (Milkweed Editions, MN, 1996).

He writes a popular, wittily idiosyncratic newspaper column, and published these "column articles" or mini essays (subtitled *Notes and objections, maximum length 43 lines*) in 1987 as *K principu rolničky*. An English edition of this book, *The Jingle Bell Principle* translated by James Naughton, was published by Bloodaxe Books in 1992.

Holub was first introduced to English readers in 1967 when Penguin published his *Selected Poems* in their Modern European Poets series, with translations by George Theiner and Ian Milner. His next two books were translated by Ian and Jarmila Milner: *Although* (Jonathan Cape, 1971) and *Notes of a Clay Pigeon* (Secker & Warburg, 1977). In America three volumes of his poetry appeared in Oberlin's Field Translation Series, translated by Stuart Friebert, David Young and Dana Hábová. In the 1970s his work was widely published in translation in English and 37 other languages, but it was not being published in Czechoslovakia, where his name had appeared on a government list, 'not for a poem, not for a book' but for signing a petition in the street. One of his poetry books was banned, others just not published; when his first book for over ten years appeared in a small edition in 1982, it sold out in a day, but could not be reprinted 'due to the paper shortage'.

In 1984 Bloodaxe Books published a selection of his poetry from the 1970s and 1980s, *On the Contrary and other poems*, translated by Ewald Osers. This brought together the poems of *Naopak*, which had been published in Prague in 1982, and a new collection, *Interferon, or On Theatre*, which was not published in Czechoslovakia until

1986, although parts of it were read or performed on stage in 1984 at Prague's Viola Poetry Theatre. Holub's poems from the 1950s and 1960s were collected in *The Fly* (Bloodaxe Books, 1987), translated by Ian & Jarmila Milner, Ewald Osers and George Theiner. His most recent collections of poems are *Vanishing Lung Syndrome*, translated by David Young (Faber & Faber, 1990), and *Supposed to Fly*, translated by Ewald Osers (Bloodaxe Books, 1996). His collected American translations (by David Young) appear in the Oberlin Translation Series in 1996, under the title *Intensive Care*.

Miroslav Holub's *Poems Before & After: Collected English Translations* (Bloodaxe Books, 1990; reissued 1995) brings together all the poems from *The Fly* and *On the Contrary*, with some additional translations. It was to have been published in this form in 1984, but the Czech authorities would not allow Holub to publish a Collected Poems in Britain. He was not a member of the Czech Writers Union, and a Collected Poems was an honour reserved for only their most distinguished writers. The book was therefore published in two halves: the second half first in 1984, and the first half second in 1987.